GUIDO CANTELLI

Guido Cantelli

Portrait of a Maestro

By

Laurence Lewis

SAN DIEGO • NEW YORK
A. S. BARNES & COMPANY, INC.
IN LONDON:
THE TANTIVY PRESS

Guido Cantelli copyright © 1981
by A.S. Barnes and Co., Inc.

First Edition
Manufactured in the United States of America

For information write to:
A.S. Barnes & Company, Inc.
P.O. Box 3051
La Jolla, California 92038

The Tantivy Press
Magdalen House
136-148 Tooley Street
London, SE1 2TT, England

Library of Congress Cataloging in Publication Data

Lewis, Laurence.
  Guido Cantelli : portrait of a maestro.

  Includes index.
  1. Cantelli, Guido. 2. Conductors (Music) —
Biography
ML422.C23L5   785'.092'4   [B]   80-29385
ISBN 0-498-02493-8

1 2 3 4 5 6 7 8 9   84 83 82 81

To my parents
Alice and Barney

Contents

"FOUR PROGRAMMES" BY GEORGINA MASE   8

ACKNOWLEDGEMENTS   9

NOVARA   11

1943–1948   29

WITH TOSCANINI   49

THE GARDEN OF MUSIC   69

APPENDIX 1:   THE PERFORMANCES   131

APPENDIX 2:   THE RECORDINGS   163

APPENDIX 3:   THE INTERVIEWS   171

BIBLIOGRAPHY   173

INDEX   174

"Four Programmes"

(for Guido Cantelli)

Genius, from the heights of vision,
Might have foreseen the universe you create:
Mountains and valleys, forests and rivers,
Waters that reflect the pageant and procession of the clouds.
Here Daphnis wanders with his Chloe;
Here the Bacchantes dance;
Here, by the pines, the Roman legions march,
Helmets gleaming where, before, moonlight
Lit the nightingale whose song sums up
Solitude, silence and dusk.
And through this world,
Pausing to smile upon the village fête,
To share the grief and merriment of simple folk,
Passing from youth to age and age to youth,
Moves Beethoven —
At one with created and creator,
Voicing, through you,
The joys and sorrows, triumphs, desires and dreams
Of all humanity.

G.M.
[Georgina Mase.]

Poem by courtesy of Iris Cantelli.

ACKNOWLEDGEMENTS

The greater part of this biographical portrait of Guido Cantelli is expressed in the words of those who knew him: musicians, friends and family, all of whom gave of their often precious moments of spare time, to share with me their memories. To them all, I would like to offer my deepest gratitude, as through them I feel I have been able in some small way to bring Guido Cantelli back to life.

In compiling the detailed listings of Cantelli's concert programmes, the following orchestras provided information relating to works performed and the dates on which they were given: Boston Symphony Orchestra (Michael Steinberg), Chicago Symphony Orchestra (Betsey Hitchcock), Philadelphia Orchestra (Florence Guion), Pittsburgh Symphony Orchestra (Mercedes Hoffman), San Francisco Symphony Orchestra (William Bernell) and Vienna Philharmonic Orchestra (Brigitta Grabner).

Similar assistance came from several of the opera houses where Cantelli worked: Teatro alla Scala, Teatro La Fenice (Antonio Busetto), The Royal Opera House, Covent Garden (B.J. Skidelsky); programme details were also obtained from the archives of the Edinburgh International Festival.

The BBC's written archives were consulted, and in connection with Cantelli's broadcast work, I must thank Mark Moersen of NBC, and Silvio Borelli of RAI.

Miss L. Kennedy of the City of Johannesburg Public Library answered my enquiry about the Johannesburg Festival by sending me copious photocopies of programmes and reviews. Through her I would like to thank the "Rand Daily Mail" and "Johannesburg Star" for allowing me to quote from their reviews.

Very little newspaper material is used in this book, and I'm grateful to the following publications for permission to reprint their writings on Cantelli: "The Scotsman," London Express News and Feature Services, for the review by Sir Beverley Baxter, which originally appeared in the "Evening Standard," "Time" for the extract from "Like I Do" (reprinted by permission from "Time, the Weekly Newsmagazine," Copyright Time Inc. 1949) and Sidney Harrison for his review of Cantelli's Festival Hall performance of *Le quattro stagioni* by Vivaldi.

There are several Cantelli discographies, but on consulting these I found they all contained errors. The one I have compiled is based on the written records kept by EMI, and I am grateful to A.R. Locantro and John Watson who made them available, and also to Peter Higgins, who provided me with valuable technical data.

Michael Robinson translated all the Italian documents that have come into my possession, whilst Luca Pfaff, Maria Teresa Esposito, Giuliano Gallini (who regarded Guido as an adopted uncle) and Professor Agostina Zecca Laterza, acted as interpreters during my researches in Italy. Professor Laterza is also Librarian of Milan Conservatory, whose archives she opened to provide the information regarding Cantelli's years of study there. I was also helped during my Italian researches by Carla Degano and Mauro Lacidogna of Propaganda Musicale, Rome.

Visiting Novara was for me a profoundly moving experience, and I should like to thank all those people of Cantelli's enchanting town whom I came into contact with, not only those directly concerned with my work, but people I met during the course of my time there. I must, though, express a tremendous debt of thanks to Professor Maria Laura Tomea, Direttrice of Novara Civic Museum, Giovani Silengo, Director of Novara State Archive, Signor Pier Luigi De Angelis, Secretary of Teatro Coccia, Signora Andreina Fasola Pelizzari and the photographer, Mario Finotti.

I must also record the assistance of: S.A.Gorlinsky, Stephen Pettitt, Mr. and Mrs. J. Heeley, Jeffrey Bacall of Alitalia's London press office, and The Arturo Toscanini Society of America.

Every researcher knows the feeling of coming across a horde of priceless material after months of painstaking sifting. When I met Stuart and Jean Agrell, this happened to me. From our first meeting, they have taken the keenest interest in my project, handing over to me documents, photographs and gramophone records. Even though I was a complete stranger when we first met, they have been generous in their hospitality, and to them I offer a very special "Thank you."

Like Stuart and Jean, Renzo Crivelli, Arts Editor of "Corriere di Novara" — the oldest local newspaper in Italy — and his delightful wife Rossella, welcomed me into their home. Renzo literally opened doors for me in Novara, arranged interviews, acted as interpreter — on one occasion with five people seated around a table, for an interview, at the end of which everyone present was sure that Guido too had been present — and proof-read my draft text on Cantelli's years in Novara. I'm pleased to call him a friend, truly without whom . . .

Laurence Lewis
Finchley, London.
January, 1979

NOVARA

"The most terrible event since La Scala was bombed during the War."
That was the immediate reaction of Dr. Antonio Ghiringhelli, Super-
intendent of Teatro alla Scala, on hearing of the death of Guido Cantelli.
He had been killed, when the plane taking him from Rome to New York
— where he was to give a season of concerts with the New York
Philharmonic Symphony Orchestra — crashed after taking off from Orly
Airport, Paris. It was November 24, 1956, and Cantelli was thirty-six
years old. Eight days earlier, La Scala had appointed Cantelli their
Musical Director, a post that had twice been occupied by Arturo
Toscanini, who said of Cantelli: "he will, I feel sure, be my true
successor."

Cantelli's first major conducting assignment took place at Teatro
Coccia, in his home town of Novara, which is situated to the north-west
of Milan, about one-third of the distance on the important communica-
tions link between there and Turin. On February 21, 1943, Cantelli
directed a performance of *La traviata* at the Coccia. Toscanini, who was
fifty-three years older than Cantelli, had on December 21, 1888, inau-
gurated the brand new Teatro Coccia by conducting *Les Huguenots*. The
season, which continued into 1889, also featured Toscanini leading
performances of *La forza del destino* and *Aida*.

Teatro Coccia stands on the remains of a previous theatre, Teatro
Nuovo, which opened in 1779 (one year after La Scala). Lavish productions of dramatic works, with accompanying music and ballet, were
the most popular entertainments of the day, through which Teatro Nuovo
earned an enviable reputation. Often the theatre played host to visiting
royalty. In 1789 the entire court of Vittorio Amedeo III, King of Sardinia
— as well as Cyprus and Jerusalem — descended on Novara for the
marriage of Vittorio Emanuele of Savoy to Princess Maris of Austria.
For the occasion Teatro Nuovo commissioned a dramatisation of the play
Enea e Lavinia with music by P.A. Guglielmi, performed by the finest
available singers and musicians. During the Risorgimento, Teatro
Nuovo's stage became a platform for expressions of Italian nationalism,
a dream which was fulfilled in 1870. Three years later on April 13,
1873, one day before his ninety-second birthday, Carlo Coccia the

A page from the programme of Toscanini's inaugural performances. Note the train timetable! Reproduced by courtesy of Signor De Angelis, Secretary, Teatro Coccia.

composer died. In his memory, Teatro Nuovo was renamed Teatro Coccia.

Despite an initial disaster with *Il matrimonio per cambiale*, Coccia's first opera heard in Rome during the 1807 season, he went on to write twenty-two operas between 1808 and 1819 that were premiered in houses all over Italy. So fast did the music flow out of Coccia's pen, that it took him only six days to write *Donna Caritea* in 1818. Around this period Coccia began to travel outside Italy, visiting Lisbon — where he composed four operas — and London. In between conducting engagements Coccia wrote *Maria Stuarda* especially for London, premiered there in 1827; he also became Professor of Composition at the Royal Academy of Music. Returning to Italy, Coccia composed one of his last theatrical works, *Caterina di Guise*, premiered at La Scala on February 14, 1833. When Mercadante relinquished the appointment of Maestro di Cappella, at the Cathedral of Novara, Coccia assumed the position in 1840. For the remainder of his life, Coccia turned his attention to writing cantatas and religious works for performance in the cathedral. He duly became one of Novara's most honoured citizens.

With the change in name from Teatro Nuovo to Teatro Coccia, a technical renovation of the building was felt to be necessary, in order to meet the requirements of contemporary theatrical needs and changing public taste. But the old theatre was found to be totally unsuitable for adaptation; a new building was needed. Money for the reconstruction was collected under the initiative of the Mayor of Novara, Marquis Luigi Tornielli, who gave through the city authorities a considerable sum that was supplemented by important citizens of Novara. Construction took two years, and from the opening in 1888, Teatro Coccia has always been regarded as one of the leading provincial theatres in northern Italy.

At no time in its history has there ever been an established company at the Coccia, such as there is at La Scala. Each season the management would bring in companies being offered by impresarios on a touring basis, with several operas receiving performances each season. These regular seasons ran until quite recently but now, at the latter end of the seventies, the Coccia is once again adapting to the needs of its audience. With the massive expense incurred by mounting operatic productions, gone are the regular seasons, and instead Teatro Coccia details its main activity throughout the year by a slight addition to its name: "Cinema Teatro Coccia."

Four operas were given during the 1943 season, opening in January with *Rigoletto* and *L'elisir d'amore*. These were conducted by Arturo Lucon, one of Teatro Coccia's most frequent musical directors around this period. More performances of *Rigoletto* took place in April, and *Il barbiere di Siviglia* joined the repertory, with yet more performances of *Rigoletto* in December. Only one other opera was given during the season — *La traviata* — and this was conducted by Guido Cantelli.

As Cantelli mounted the podium, a chorus of encouragement erupted from the gallery of the packed theatre. "Bravo, Maestro!" Guido's friends were calling. "Go on, Cantelli!" "Ciao, Guido!" they cried. Facing the orchestra, baton raised, the twenty-two year-old conductor waited until silence enveloped the audience, before making the gestures through which the Prelude to Act One cast its spell over the theatre.

*

Novara lies in the centre of the Po Valley, whose fertile soil makes the area ideal for cultivating rice. However, the crop is not brought to market in Novara but Vercelli, a short distance to the north-west, between Novara and Turin. By road from Novara, one passes through Borgo Vercelli, a suburb of Vercelli so small it scarcely registers as more than a place name. It was here on July 11, 1884, that Guido Cantelli's mother, Angela Riccardone was born. The Riccardones owned a bar or restaurant (no one can remember which), but they sold the business and moved to Novara. Here they opened a grocery store, with living accommodation above the shop. A frequent customer was Antonio Cantelli, attracted not only by the produce but also by the Riccardones' pretty daughter Angela, who served behind the counter. Like the Riccardones, the Cantellis were not natives of Novara; they hailed from Galliera near Ferrara, where Antonio was born on January 17, 1879.

Pursuing a career as a regular soldier and military bandsman with the Seventeenth Artillery Regiment, who were stationed in Novara, Antonio played the horn and trumpet in the regimental band. Eventually Antonio became their bandmaster, which meant that he was in command of all musical matters pertaining to the band and regiment. With his new position went the rank of Marshal (equivalent to Sergeant). In this rank, Antonio served in the First World War, receiving several good conduct medals. He also possessed a fine tenor voice, which he grossly under-rated, never singing in public, but only for family and friends. Angela Riccardone was captivated by the dashing young soldier-musician, whose concerts with the regimental band she attended by special invitation of the conductor. Off-duty and in each other's company, Antonio and Angela joined in musical *soirés* at friends' houses. They married in Novara on April 30, 1912.

After their marriage Antonio and Angela Cantelli set up home in a ground-floor apartment at Via San Guadenzio 19. The faded, ochre-coloured house is reached through a grey stone courtyard entrance almost opposite the great square portal of the Basilica di San Guadenzio. Consecrated in 1659, the building is capped by Alessandro Antonelli's extraordinary wedding-cake cupola, completed after twenty-four years in 1888: at 121 metres, it is the tallest structure built in bricks without concrete support. The Basilica's environs would play an important role in the formative years of Guido Cantelli's musical education. At least these years would be secure, as Antonio's military career gave the Cantellis a stable base on which to live and bring up their family. "If I could have 1,000 lire a month . . . I will be happy," ran a line from a current popular song. Antonio received 1,200!

Seven years separated Guido from his older brother Giuseppe, the only other child of the Cantellis' marriage. Guido was born in the apartment at Via San Gaudenzio 19, on April 27, 1920. With his arrival this became too small, and the family moved to the apartment directly above, which was considerably larger. "There was a lot of music about the house," recalled Giuseppe Cantelli. "I used to play a violin and Guido the piano. He started playing the piano when he was six or seven, and gave small concerts for the family."

Guido had begun to take an interest in music before he could read or write. How could the child not fail to have been stimulated, when he saw his father in uniform leading the band, of which he soon became unofficial mascot? Antonio would take Guido with him when he conducted a band at nearby Vespolate and, watching, Guido began to imitate his father's gestures with the baton; surely it must be a magic wand to produce those sounds from the musicians? There could be no greater treat for the five-year-old Guido than to be taken by his father to a band rehearsal. As Antonio worked, Guido looked on entranced, and began once again to imitate his father. Seeing this, Antonio stood Guido on a chair, giving him the baton. Immediately the band came to life, intoxicating Guido with the thought that through his baton the sounds were being produced as if by some alchemy that flowed through the stick. What an impact that must have made! Actually Antonio, supporting Guido on his chair, was giving the musicians their cues from behind his son's back. Later, Antonio wanted Guido to become a member of the band, and for about a year he flirted with trumpets and cornets, but he already knew that his father's field of music-making had severe limitations, and that his musical inclinations were veering in a totally different direction.

Music never became for Giuseppe as important as it was obviously becoming for Guido. He played his violin for relaxation, but together with his brother they made a more than accomplished duo: only a cellist was needed to form a perfect trio. On the day that Guido was born, nine-year-old Angelo Bernasconi was allowed to look at the new-born baby. Angelo's parents lived in another apartment at number nineteen, and as soon as Guido became responsive he and Angelo became friends. The difference in their ages was no bar to friendship, as Angelo too had a great love of music and he played an instrument — the cello.

A trio was formed and Guido very quickly began to assert himself. Angelo Bernasconi vividly remembered: "We started to play together when Guido was seven or eight. We would talk about technical problems, and when Guido was eight he told us, 'Do like that; play like this, you've got to play as I want to.'" Antonio, if time permitted, would sit and listen to these sessions, but according to Angelo Bernasconi: "He was very pleased when we used to play, but he didn't say a word, just stayed there and listened — then he went." The bandmaster offered no words of advice.

As a professional musician, Antonio could see that his youngest son possessed an extraordinary gift for music, which needed to be channelled properly. Clearly the boy had reached a stage of development where he would be responsive to professional musical tuition. This was something Antonio could not give, he had neither the time, nor — more importantly — the qualifications. Antonio could instil a love and respect of music, and the discipline of interpreting it. Only a qualified tutor could devote the necessary time to ascertaining Guido's true musical inclinations, and developing them to their fullest extent. Guido was taken to Maestro Felice Fasola, Organist and Director of the Choir, at the Basilica di San Gaudenzio.

*

Under Felice Fasola, Guido received a solid foundation upon which to build his future career. Until that time no one suspected the boy possessed a voice of suitable quality to warrant applying for a junior chorister's position. Yet Fasola's first task on being presented with Guido as a pupil had been to test his voice, which he found secure in intonation, thus almost by default gaining him entry into the Basilica's choir. (Incidentally, Guido retained the ability to sing in a high register until his early twenties.) Musically, San Gaudenzio's choir never lapsed into routine, as Fasola gave them music from all periods to perform during services. It was a medium he personally loved, composing over the years twenty-two "Ave Maria," three "Salve Regina" and thirty-seven Motets, all receiving performances at the Basilica.

For the first time, Guido came into contact through the choir with a group of people all making music towards a united goal. Watching Antonio's band, Guido could see each musician playing their part in creating a unified musical concept, welded together by their conductor. No musician — however gifted — merited the right to go off at a tangent, thereby destroying that concept. Inside San Gaudenzio's choir, Guido realised that each member contributed to the overall impact, which could be lessened by a weak link or by one member's antipathy towards their director. Perfection could only be achieved when all were as one, and only perfection was good enough.

Privately with Fasola, Guido's piano studies took up the greater part of their time together. Fasola also saw how Guido had been thrilled by the sound of San Gaudenzio's organ, and took his young pupil through his first halting encounters with the console and pedals. Fasola also encouraged Cantelli's youthful compositions: at the age of ten, Guido composed a Mass dedicated to his parents, which Fasola thought good enough for a public performance; this took place at the Basilica, under the composer's direction. When Cantelli appeared at the 1955 Edinburgh Festival, conducting the New York Philharmonic Symphony Orchestra, he confessed in an interview published in "The Scotsman's" festival diary, that at thirty-five he did not like being called a "young conductor," since he had first played the organ of his church and directed the choir when he was eight. That meant he had been conducting for twenty-seven years! This statement (assuming it was taken down correctly) suggests that the time locked itself in Guido's memory through some particular event, and that joining the choir brought forth Guido's musical attributes, which needed only a spark to ignite. On Cantelli's own words, together with those of Angelo Bernasconi, it appears that he did indeed begin to assert his musical personality around the age of eight.

Certainly, Fasola realised early on that Cantelli was no run-of-the-mill pupil, but gifted to an extraordinary degree. (Fasola later regarded Cantelli as his most intelligent pupil.) As such, Fasola nurtured Cantelli by giving him extra work to study and perform. Felice Fasola had studied piano in Novara and composition in Milan, obtaining a diploma in piano at the Regio Liceo Musicale in Bologna. From 1915 until 1958 — a year before his death at the age of eighty-six — Fasola held the position at San Gaudenzio. A former pupil of Fasola's, Folco Perrino (at the time of writing in 1978 Professor of Piano at Antonio Vivaldi Conservatory, Alessandria) offered this assessment of Felice Fasola's musicianship: "He was a good provincial teacher in the best sense of the word. He wasn't very keen on piano; his outlook was more general. He was a good teacher — no more than that — and not at the level of a conservatory." Although several years younger than Cantelli, Folco Perrino became friendly with him from their first meeting, in the years leading up to the outbreak of war. Did he think Fasola exerted a great influence on Cantelli, at a time when he was receptive to many musical stimuli? "He was so talented that of course Fasola did not influence him directly. Some things Guido could have picked up from him, just small pointers."

As Guido Cantelli became a teenager, the duties he performed at San Gaudenzio took on more and more the role of assistant to Fasola. When he was fourteen or fifteen, Guido began to act as a substitute if Fasola could not attend a service; he then played the organ and directed the choir. Only one actual date on which Cantelli played the organ at San Gaudenzio appears to be documented. On January 22, 1943, the feast of the patron saint of San Gaudenzio was celebrated by a solemn mass. The choir sang Perosi's *Missa benedicamus domino*, and Cantelli's organ accompaniment is described as being played with great technical security. Word soon got around about San Gaudenzio's young substitute organist, who began to receive invitations to substitute at other churches in Novara. For a time he played in at least two churches on this basis;

one of these, the Madonna del Carmine, stands in Via dei Cattaneo, a short distance from San Gaudenzio.

Adjoining the Madonna del Carmine is the Istituto Suore Giuseppine, a private primary school run by nuns, which Guido attended from the age of five. At nine he passed to a junior school, the Galileo Ferraris, where he astonished his teacher by taking over a singing class. He drew the musical stave on the blackboard, taught the notes to his classmates, then proceeded to conduct them. When Guido sat an "eleven plus" examination he received the following marks: Italian Language 7, General Culture 7, Physical Education 6, Arithmetic 8, Design (Drawing) 7. These were sufficient to earn a first grade diploma, awarded on June 22, 1931. This gained him entry to the R. [*Regio*] Istituto Tecnico "O.F. Mossotti" sited on Via Curtatone, where it is still. The course laid great emphasis on commerce, equipping the students for careers in banking and clerical work — skills that Guido would one day put to use.

School never became an intermission between musical activities, as Guido took a genuine interest in all the subjects put before him. Of all the lessons learnt during those years, perhaps most important to his future was one that did not even appear on the curriculum: how never to stop learning. Right through his life Guido searched and probed, looking for the truth in a work of music, as he saw it. Never afraid to listen to what those older and more experienced than him offered by way of interpretative insights, he would then apply their thoughts to his own, to re-define in his own terms exactly what he was seeking. "He was very good at maths, and I presume that's the reason why he was very good in music." (Giuseppe Cantelli)

As music consumed Guido Cantelli and those precious childhood years, there were never, apart from Angelo, many friends upon whom Guido would call. Despite being part of San Gaudenzio's musical establishment, outside its ambience Guido's mind raced along on a plane that made ordinary boyhood friendships impossible for him. Giuseppe Cantelli witnessed the effect of this on Guido: "I remember seeing my brother sitting in corners thinking about music." He knew where he was going, but as yet the distance was too great for an exact goal to be in sight. Guido's personality had sufficiently formed for him to know that although he would never be one of the crowd, this was not too great a sacrifice to make for the sake of his ultimate goal.

Possibly Guido thought that the piano would take an important role in his future, for it assumed great importance for him. "He used to play the piano for many hours, particularly in the evening. Because he did not want to disturb the family, he put something like rags into the piano, to keep it more silent." (Giuseppe Cantelli.)

Opportunities for Guido to perform his piano repertoire in public frequently occurred in Novara. These took the form of musical evenings, known to have included a performance at the Associazione Mutilati di

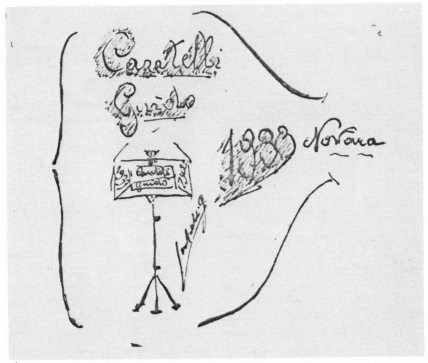

Sketch by Guido. Reproduced by courtesy of Mariangela Cantelli.

Guerra di Novara (an ex-serviceman's club) and one in the Broletto (Mayor's Palace), one of Novara's oldest buildings, dating from the Fourteenth century. Coincidentally, Guido was fourteen when these performances were given, the extent of his repertoire being:

Liszt: *Hungarian Rhapsody No. 2*
Beethoven: Piano Sonata No. 14 "Moonlight"
Musorgsky: "Baba Yaga" and "The Great Gate of Kiev" from *Pictures at an Exhibition*
Wagner: "Vorspiel und Liebestod": *Tristan und Isolde* Overture: *Tannhäuser*

Only selections were performed, as of course Guido shared the platform with other musicians. Not until the darkest period of the war did he give his only formal recital.

With a growing repertoire came a burgeoning library of scores, of which some were purchased at Olivieri's music shop on Novara's Corso Cavour. At the same time Guido discovered, in Milan, an Aladdin's cave of music at Gallini's. Situated on the corner of Corso Monforte and Via del Conservatorio, at the end of which stands Milan Conservatory, Gallini's have been at their present address since 1928, and a family business since their foundation in 1888. When Guido first called at the shop around 1936 or 1937, Natale Gallini managed affairs. Natale's son

Giuseppe at once struck up a friendship with Guido, who was two years older — a friendship brought to an end only by Cantelli's death. "At sixteen or seventeen," recalled Giuseppe Gallini, he looked like someone more grown than they really were." Gallini continued:

> He used to spend many many hours looking into old scores. I never felt that Guido hadn't enough money to buy scores; he was extremely regular and well ordered in buying. He used to buy only what he could afford; from this point-of-view he was very bright minded. He had a sharp interest in practically all periods of music. I cannot say that he preferred a certain period in comparison to any other.

If Guido's repertoire, enumerated earlier, contained a proportion of orchestral music in piano reduction, this was simply because for someone in Guido's position the piano offered the best way of studying these works in detail. Symphony concerts were never given in Novara; Milan, on the other hand, presented a rich diet of music in the immediate prewar years. Regular orchestral seasons were held in the spring and summer at La Scala, and there was a winter season given in the large concert hall of the conservatory. Giuseppe Gallini remembered attending these concerts, sometimes accompanied by Guido, and they must be accounted his first experiences of live orchestral music.

A seat at La Scala, either for an opera or concert, was far beyond anything Guido could afford, but a seat in the gallery at Teatro Coccia amounted to only a few hundred lire. Their prewar seasons were entirely devoted to Italian opera, as a glance through the programme indicates:

1936–March: *Lucia di Lammermoor.*
1936–1937: *Tosca; Rigoletto.*
1937–March: *La traviata.*
1937–May: *Don Pasquale.*
1937–1938: *Mefistofele; La bohème; La Gioconda;*
			Il piccolo Marat (Mascagni).
1938–1939: *La forza del destino; La Wally;*
			Notturno romantico (Pick-Mangiagalli); *Cavalleria rusticana;*
			Madama Butterfly; Turandot.

Nothing exists detailing exactly which performances Cantelli attended; he is, however, vividly recalled sitting in the gallery. While all eyes inside Teatro Coccia were focused on stage, Guido would be attempting to follow the opera from a score held on his lap, and illuminated by a torch! This brought an understanding of the complexities involved in an operatic performance, and they began to overpower Guido. To Giuseppe Gallini he confided that he did not feel strong enough to conduct opera, and he considered opera the most difficult kind of music to direct. For Guido, at this stage of his development, any experience of live music was to be treasured, even though he now had a way of supplementing this with a range of music far in excess of anything the combined efforts of Milan and Novara could offer — radio.

*

Despite the magnificent strides made in recording technique during the 1930's, no matter how sophisticated a reproducer was employed, gramophone recordings were bedevilled by their limitation of five minutes duration per twelve-inch side. Listening in a domestic situation inevitably lead to gaps in musical continuity as sides were changed. Radio could partly overcome that, by playing works running to more than one side in a sequence. More importantly, microphones were now sensitive enough to be placed in concert halls and opera houses, with the result that for the first time people unable to attend a live performance could participate in the experience — and listen uninterrupted.

Hardly a night went by when Guido would not spend several hours listening to his father's radio, tuning up and down the wavebands trying to find a station broadcasting a work not encountered before. Some works received more air time than others and those which caught Guido's imagination were added to his library. Now as he listened and followed with the score, the work's shape and form became apparent as the notes were transformed into sounds. Often these would be drowned by interference — particularly if he was tuned to a distant transmitter — and by the fact that Antonio's radio was not capable of handling full orchestral tone. From his small allowance, Guido each week for months put by a small sum until he had enough to purchase a radiogram, responsive enough to satisfy its listener. Straight away Guido's treasure assumed an awed position in the Cantellis' living room, as its beautiful wooden cabinet poured forth the most thrilling of sounds. (It still works, being in the possession of Guido's niece Mariangela Cantelli.) With the radiogram came an opportunity to collect records, and to study those works previously heard broadcast, which could now be gone into in far greater depth. Like his scores the record library grew quickly, Guido being a frequent browser at Olivieri's. Recordings conducted by Toscanini figured among those purchased, Guido little knowing that one day he would listen to them in the presence of the Maestro, on *his* radiogram!

For the moment though, Guido shared these pleasures with Sergio Scarpa, a friend his own age, whom he met on a cold and rainy day in Milan. Hurrying to catch a train for Novara, Guido's attention became attracted by the sound of a familiar symphonic theme drifting out of an open window. He began to whistle it quietly to himself, at the same time as Sergio, approaching from across the road, began whistling it too, and for a moment they whistled in unison. Sergio introduced himself, telling

Guido he was an accountancy student; it transpired that he too lived in Novara, so as they were getting rather wet, Guido suggested that they make their way to the station. Sergio also listened devotedly to his radio at night, with the result that by the time they had reached Novara an unusual arrangement had been arrived at. Following an evening of listening, Guido or Sergio would call at each other's houses with news of what they had heard. Occasionally a first performance would be broadcast and, unable to wait until their appointed meeting time, Guido or Sergio could be seen running through the streets to tell each other of their good fortune.

Sergio had an open invitation to the Cantelli household, spending hours with Guido listening to the radio and playing records. For a time Sergio even joined with Guido, Giuseppe and Angelo, to make a very happy quartet; but already Guido was beginning to leave Sergio far behind in his musical quest. In fact, Guido's invitations to Sergio to come and listen to important broadcasts began to be refused. At first Guido thought Sergio must be ill, only after a time realising that something more lay behind these constant refusals. Calling on Sergio, Guido received a shock — as the front door was opened, he saw another figure standing beside his friend — a girl! Sergio introduced her as Maria, to whom he was shortly to become engaged. This stunning fact of life proved too much for Guido, who could not comprehend that his friend should be taken away from him by a woman. It was something completely unexpected. Excusing himself, Guido rushed home.

Somehow — it is not very clear how — Guido heard that a jazz band playing a summer season at the Hotel Grande Bretagne at Bellagio, the resort on Lake Como, required a pianist. Guido applied and got the job. After such a traumatic upheaval he needed time to think, a complete break with routine appeared to be an ideal way of solving this dilemma. If nothing else came out of these unfamiliar musical surroundings, the opportunity had arisen to try and instill his own standards in a group of musicians. Those summer months of 1937 were hardly the most stimulating of Guido's life, but as the pounding rhythms (the aspect of jazz which appealed most to Guido) filled his mind, he began to see that there was more to life than the narrow confines of the existence that he had created for himself in Novara.

Like all young Italians, Guido belonged to the Fascist youth movement. Apart from acting as an instrument of political indoctrination, it maintained a large and varied cultural programme, each year organising a choral competition featuring regional winners from all over Italy, with a final held in Rome. Guido took part in this competition, but very little detailed information exists to say how long he was connected with the choir in Novara. It appears unlikely that Guido brought about the choir's genesis, which in all probability had existed for some time, being organised by party officials, Guido becoming its conductor by a process of natural selection, or through his work at San Gaudenzio —Fasola may well have put in a word in his favour. Rehearsals took place on Sunday afternoon — possibly in San Guadenzio — with Guido's choice of music: Palestrina, Victoria, Monteverdi, Gabrieli, Frescobaldi, Carissimi and Lassus, reflecting his work at the Basilica.

Each choir entering the competition had to prepare a test piece, *La montanara* an alpine folk-song, arranged by Achille Eschinelli, who arrived in person to audition Guido's choir. After the performance, Eschinelli motioned Guido over to him. Emphatically he told Guido that his tempo must be slower and broader, but as he was inviting the choir to Rome, between now and the finals they could under the conductor's guidance arrive at the correct tempo. As Eschinelli departed, Guido turned to his one-hundred-strong choir muttering "cretino," knowing that his tempo not the composer's was correct. At the final in May (it is difficult to put an exact date on this as no two sources agree, but the period 1939 to 1941 represents the closest approximation), Cantelli's interpretation of *La montanara* superbly realised, did not differ in any way from that heard by Eschinelli in January. Again Eschinelli motioned Cantelli over to his side and in front of the other judges and audience publicly reproved him — although expressing admiration for his inter-pretations, and the choir's rendering of the remainder of their programme — for not heeding his instructions over *La montanara*. As a result, they were not to be the winners, but placed among the runners up.

*

In 1940, the Cantelli family moved to a new apartment at Via Alessandro Antonelli 1. Their new house faced squarely the facade of San Guadenzio.

A remarkable document survives from this time, just one foolscap sheet — little more than a piece of scrap — dated May 17. On it Guido, now aged twenty, has drafted what appears to be the lay-out of a huge symphony orchestra; dotted about the page are several attempts at perfecting a signature; what makes it unique, however, are the thoughts Guido has written: "Some people define love as an auto-suggestion, and so little of will is enough to wake them up. I, on the contrary, define love as the pure will of soul, and so only auto-suggestion could touch it."

Coming from one whose romantic proclivities were confined to falling in love with the girl across the street or sitting opposite in the bus or train, this statement about the meaning of love was clearly sparked off by something more than one of Guido's "brief encounters." Normally Guido's reticence put a wall of silence between him and any girl he was attracted to, but could these words have been prompted by the one occasion when he did manage to break through?

Guido had caught the attention of Iris Bilucaglia, who sat facing him during a journey from Novara to Milan. As usual Iris had woken

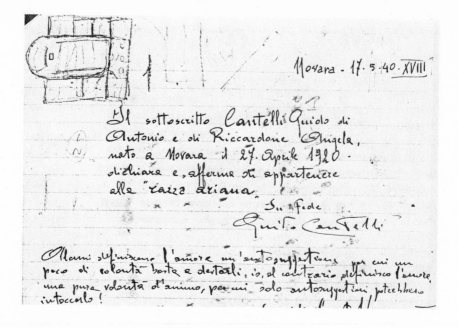

A detail from the document mentioned on previous page. Reproduced by courtesy of Mariangela Cantelli.

late, dashed through breakfast and arrived just in time to catch the train. On most days she spent the journey revising the previous day's notes, ready for another day's study at Milan's Brera Institute. On this particular morning the notes lay open, unread. Iris gazed at Guido, dressed in a maroon coat, underneath which could be seen a grey suit. All thoughts of her art studies forgotten, Iris tried to place the face of the man sitting opposite, engrossed in a page of music. Guido perhaps noticed her quizzical expression, for he pre-empted her by asking: "Excuse me, Signorina, it seems we have met somewhere before." This time-honoured phrase caught Iris off guard, and she thought it a prelude to an early morning pick-up. Then in a flash, the pieces coalesced in her mind — Cantelli! Guido Cantelli!! The Cantelli she had performed with in 1930, during a school play, Guido in the role of leading actor (who sang when required), she as a ballerina. It all came flooding back: services at the Basilica when Guido had substituted for Maestro Fasola, playing the love theme from *Tristan und Isolde* (given at the Coccia during the 1935–1936 season) during the elevation of the host, and later in the service the march from Tchaikovsky's Sixth Symphony. As they parted on Milan Central station, Iris wondered if Guido would be there the following morning. He was — and thereafter on each day that his studies took him to Milan, Guido waited for Iris on the platform at Novara. For them both a journey was beginning that would reach heights of ecstasy, to culminate in shattering tragedy.

Soon they began to see each other in the evenings, but their obviously growing relationship brought strictures from Iris's parents, whose response to Guido at their first meeting was decidedly cool, since they did not want her to become involved with anyone, fearing it would detract from her studies. They could see that Guido was an honest boy but he was dedicated to a career as a professional musician, and in their opinion could never hope to provide for Iris in the style she had been brought up to expect. Against this background Guido and Iris found they could not be without each other's company — literally Iris was Guido's only love.

*

Just as Guido had soon reached the limits of his father's musical knowledge so, in time, further study with Fasola became a fruitless exercise. Fasola could offer Guido no further means of developing as a musician. In Folco Perrino's opinion: "Fasola realised that Guido Cantelli knew much more than he did!" Only intensive study at a conservatory would be of benefit to Guido now, and Fasola recommended a course at Milan.

Entering Conservatorio di Musica "Giuseppe Verdi" Milano, as a composition student, Guido began formal classes on August 20, 1939. In the first year his teachers were Adolfo Bossi and Arrigo Pedrollo. When examinations were held in June 1940, Guido scored eight-and-a-half marks out of a possible ten.

Switching teachers, Cantelli joined the class of Giorgio Federico Ghedini (1892–1965). Ghedini's course lasted seven years, but it took Guido only three years to complete it. Several factors could account for this: for a prodigy seven years were not necessary or, as appears more probable, the course had to be shortened or curtailed because of wartime conditions. There is no way to be absolutely certain, as the conservatory's archives were extensively damaged in the Milan air raids, and everything they contain on Cantelli is included here. At the conclusion of the three year period 1940–1943, Cantelli again received eight-and-a-half marks out of ten.

A lifelong friendship developed between Cantelli and Ghedini, who dedicated several works to his pupil. Ghedini was a noted authority on Italian Baroque music, preparing modern performing editions which Cantelli included in concerts throughout his career. It is likely that Ghedini stimulated Cantelli's interest in this period and made him recognise the importance of these compositions in the Italian musical heritage.

Bearing in mind the amount of time Cantelli spent with Ghedini, both inside and out of the conservatory, how great a part did the older man play in shaping Cantelli artistically? Giuseppe Gallini knew Ghedini throughout his years at the conservatory — latterly as director: "In my opinion, not a very great influence. We can speak more about a technical influence, than any other kind of influence. Cantelli could have succeeded with any master, it didn't make any difference if he was a pupil of Ghedini, or of someone else."

Between 1941 and 1942, Antonino Votto gave the first conducting course ever to be given at the conservatory. As a student of composition, Cantelli gained automatic entry. The form of the course was outlined by Maestro Votto:

> These courses [Antonino Votto continued teaching at the conservatory until 1967] were theoretical. Practical being made up of technical notions of gestures; of lectures on piano pieces and generally of orchestral exercises, which culminated in compositions from which came varied symphonic music concerts of accompaniament from Mozart to Beethoven, and sometimes with more modern writings — a concerto for cello and orchestra of Malipiero and others.
>   Guido Cantelli showed from the first a mastery of music and its techniques.

During the course, Cantelli directed three concerts (or shared the podium with other students), in February, April and May 1942, with an orchestra comprised of students and professors of the conservatory. Works by Vivaldi and Rossini featured in these programmes, whilst in the final concert Guido included a composition of his own: *Theme with Variations.* According to Antonino Votto it was "very successful," yet although it was formally and technically correct, Cantelli felt that it did not say anything musically significant. It did, however, become a decisive factor in pointing Cantelli away from composition and towards interpretation. The year under Antonino Votto convinced Cantelli that conducting was the outlet for his musical talents he had long been seeking.

Graduating on February 3, 1943, with a diploma in composition, Guido immediately received a call for military service, only to be rejected on this occasion due to thoracic insufficiency. It meant a reprieve long enough to give him the first great public test of his career.

*

As the effects of the war made themselves felt, the major opera houses found it increasingly difficult to operate and reluctantly had to close, releasing a great number of singers who at first found themselves without work. Teatro Coccia, not having its own company was able to keep open throughout the war years, presenting occasional performances when these became available through impresarios. A search of the theatre's archive, however, produced nothing relating to any of the productions mounted in the period 1941–1945, and nothing whatsoever on Guido Cantelli, any written records having presumably been destroyed during those chaotic years. How Cantelli came to be offered the chance to conduct *La traviata* is, then, somewhat shrouded in mystery. One theory that has been advanced is that an impresario offered the production and Teatro Coccia's management, knowing of Cantelli's recent graduation, wanted as an act of faith to give him an important engagement to prove himself. Of course there were arguments the impresario wanting his conductor — possibly Arturo Lucon — rather than an unknown musician with no operatic experience, but the Coccia stood firm, giving Cantelli his chance.

Because the production was a revival it had to be mounted in only a couple of days, robbing Guido of precious rehearsal time, not even a dress rehearsal being possible. Dress caused one minor problem, as until now Guido had never required an evening suit. With all his energies concentrated on the music, he thought the conductor automatically appeared in his suit of tails! Fortunately he was directed to an address in Milan, where these could be hired, and so this matter was quickly resolved.

February 21st saw Teatro Coccia alive with excitement. Working in an orchestra pit for the first time, Guido experienced the dislocating sensation of watching his singers opening their mouths, but not actually being able to hear what came out. The orchestra simply drowned their voices, giving an impression of gesticulating marionettes.

During the second interval, Teatro Coccia's management laid on a small reception. Iced champagne flowed plentifully, with Guido freely indulging. Ghedini, proud of his pupil's performance, emptied a glass over Guido's head as a token of esteem. Returning to conduct Act Three, Guido found the champagne had truly gone to his head, as the entire score had vanished from his memory. "They got me drunk, I can't remember how Act Three starts," Cantelli whispered to the musicians directly in front of him. When a musician suggested fetching a copy of the score, the gravity of the situation was enough to instantly restore Guido's memory. At the final curtain, a torrent of applause burst forth which seemed to last forever. The audience were telling Cantelli that he had more than justified the management's faith in him and that with this performance his artistic credibility was proven beyond doubt, both to his fellow artistes, and to himself.

As yet, however, this triumph was to be an isolated one for, as Guido Cantelli's hand put down the baton on the last page of Verdi's score, it would be replaced by a rifle.

1943-1948

Once again Cantelli was summoned to do his military service, and on this occasion to become a subject of medical controversy. Two doctors, one a major and a regular soldier, the other a conscript, could not agree about Cantelli's eligibility for service. The conscript understood how he felt about being pressganged into Mussolini's army and recommended the usual three-month discharge; to the major, however, Cantelli appeared perfectly fit. While they argued, another doctor arrived from Turin, and assurred Cantelli that military service would make him stronger, thereby settling the issue, with Cantelli facing the inevitable drafting into army service.

*

German troops occupied Rome on September 11, 1943, marking the eventual seizure of northern Italy. That same day, the government of Marshal Pietro Badoglio, which had ousted Mussolini, declared war on Germany and moved south to be with the advancing allied armies, who, under General Mark Clark of the U.S. Fifth Army, had made their first landing on the Italian peninsula at Salerno on September 9. On the previous day, soldiers of the Third Reich had marched into Novara, which became their centre of field operations for the region of Piedmont.

Previous comments about Cantelli's deportation, state categorically that he was deported as an anti-fascist, but the Germans in fact simply offered the Italians the choice of either fighting with them against the Allies or, if they declined, a sentence in a labour camp. The Germans were desperately short of manual workers to build defences and the Italians, soldiers or civilians, could provide a workforce. It seems unlikely that each person was asked if they were sympathetic to the German cause: here was a source of men, resident in barracks; on the streets — it mattered little which, and, Cantelli included, they were rounded up.

A terrible journey followed, the final destination being Stettin on the Baltic coast. Here Cantelli was forced to do heavy manual labour in the open air, in bitterly cold winds blowing in from the sea. Food was scarce and Guido's weight dropped to a dangerously low level, with the little sustenance derived from what did come his way very quickly dissipated by the constant work and ever-present cold. In that moment of supreme crisis, a change of mind by the Germans led to the Italians being moved to an asylum near Stuttgart.

Conditions were little better: Guido still received no medical attention and was unable to keep any food down, even though it contained rather more than the scraps he had previously been fed. Having exhausted the Italians physically, the Germans now began a mental assault. Mussolini was ensconced in the town of Salò, on Lake Garda, where the Germans had created for him an artificial fascist state controlling northern Italy — known to posterity as the Salò Republic. The Germans hoped that *Il Duce's* call to arms would bring forth sufficient support to replenish depletions caused by the Allied advances. Morale at Stuttgart grew very low as the Italians did not know for what purpose they were being held. As uncertainty prevailed, an offer of repatriation, conditional on signing to fight with the Salò fascists (the "Repubblichini" as they were contemptuously called — the troops of the "little" Republic of Salò, fighting against unarmed people), came as a way of getting back to Italy. Cantelli signed, declaring that he believed in the programme of the new-born Republic, and found himself on board a train heading for Italy.

The standard biographical note on Guido Cantelli is quite explicit in portraying him as completely untainted in any way by fascism. It is possible to deduce exactly why this laundered version, most likely cooked up by some overanxious PR men in America, has over the years become accepted as truth and ultimately myth. One word tells all: Toscanini. With Cantelli becoming so closely associated with Toscanini, he needed to be shown as, politically, absolutely clean. Toscanini had of course publicly expressed his loathing of Mussolini, which led to his being virtually hounded out of Italy. Nor could Cantelli afford to be associated with the left, since his first appearances in America coincided with the era of Senator Joe McCarthy's notorious witch hunts. In truth, Cantelli was neither a Fascist or a Marxist, and had no interest in politics at all. The only politics that really excited Guido were the internal machinations at La Scala, and he would keep Toscanini amused over the dinner table on his visits to New York with graphic accounts of the latest scandals.

On the train, with its limited space and incessant jolting, Cantelli, utterly exhausted, slipped into unconsciousness, being spared the floor by a makeshift hammock. It was obvious he would not survive the journey to Italy without medical attention. Reaching Bolzano on the Italian/Swiss border, the train halted and those too ill to continue were taken off by "Repubblichini" for hospitalisation. The hospital was more like a prison as there were little or no facilities for treatment and sleep was impossible due to the sound of constant gunfire. What medicines were available consisted entirely of vitamins, which Guido received in large doses, producing the side effect of making him appear to grow very large. With so few nursing staff, Guido's mind began turning on what might happen next: faced with the probability that he would be sent to fight thoughts of escape became uppermost in his mind.

The hospital chaplain paid regular visits to Cantelli's bedside. When it emerged in conversation that Cantelli played the organ he was asked if he would like to play on the harmonium in the hospital chapel. Cantelli whiled away a short time each day in this way, ever alert to the fact that at any moment he might be declared fit. At one of his sessions the chaplain, after making a comment on his choice of music, suprised Cantelli by saying that he despised the Fascists and would help him to escape. Leading him behind the altar, the chaplain pointed out a door, saying that when he next came to play, he should open the door, where he would find civilian clothes, a Red Cross arm-band and a few thousand lire. At the far end of the passageway another door opened on to the street where, leaning against the wall, a bicycle would be standing — the rest was up to him. In this manner, Cantelli effected an escape from Bolzano. Travelling mostly by night, he reached Novara in late 1943 or early 1944. At the most, Cantelli had been away four months, but he carried the marks of those experiences for the rest of his life, a permanent legacy being lumbago.

There could be no question of a return to music, as Guido's physical and mental states were totally unprepared for the rigours of a performance. Understanding assistance in helping him return to a normal life came from the director of the Banca Popolare di Novara, with an offer of employment. For three months he worked in the bank processing cheques, the bank's personnel records being doctored to make it appear that he had been an employee since 1942. Cantelli lived quite openly, at no time under an assumed name. A misconception which stems from this period is that Cantelli fought with the partisans. In fact, although he never took part in raids he did assist Sergio Scarpa, who worked for them, in procuring forged documents and attending to administrative work.

An opportunity of picking up the threads of his career came with two performances of *La Bohème* at Biella, north of Vercelli, on March 25/26, 1944. Although he was unready as yet to unleash his full musical powers these performances offered a foundation on which to rebuild. Unfortunately Guido caught acute bronchitis and conducted with a high fever. Combined with his still poor physical state, this meant that he had to be supported to the podium, then carried back to his dressing room at the close of each act virtually in a faint. Ill though he was, Guido refused to hand over the baton, and as soon as the music began he was transformed into the complete musical master.

A re-engagement at Teatro Coccia followed, with performances of *Madama Butterfly, Werther* and *La traviata* scheduled for April and May. Contemporary reviews are not very detailed, but Cantelli's *Werther* was acknowledged to be a triumph of natural sound, with applause breaking out after the aria *Ah non mi Ridestar*. Folco Perrino attended *Werther* and *La traviata* and although he cannot now remember any particular details about these performances, he still retains an overall impression: "I remember having a particular feeling realizing a man aged twenty [sic] that could direct like that, understanding the music so deeply. I felt a sort of trembling, when you feel something great is happening."

Cantelli worked with highly experienced Italian singers, some of whom were taking roles they had cultivated over an entire career. With a young and, to them, inexperienced conductor in the pit the danger existed of a headstrong singer taking over the performance. But this did not happen, as Perrino recalls: "it was impossible, because he had already developed completely his personality. They couldn't do anything against him, they had to obey his orders."

A few days after the *Traviata* performances, Cantelli received a letter from Margherita Carosio, who had taken the role of Violetta:

                                                    Milan 24th May 1944

Dear Maestro Cantelli,

Whilst I am sending you my photograph, I would like to ask you very warmly to take charge yourself of the sending of the other one which you will find enclosed in "Il popolo Novarese." Your musical interpretation of *Traviata* will always be carried by me in my soul and the short words of my dedication quite properly express my profound conviction of the inevitable great future which you have ahead of you.

If you should come to Milan, I should be very pleased to see you again and to spend an hour with you, and in the meantime I beg you to accept the expression of my admiring friendship.

                                                    Margherita Carosio

Eight months were to elapse before Cantelli conducted again. He resumed his position at the bank on a temporary basis which allowed him time for study, in preparation for a piano recital. Given in Novara during November, the recital contained works by Chopin, Beethoven, Weber and Liszt. As he played, Guido drew the audience close to him, communicating in a few brief instants of time a sense that life had returned to normal.

1944, was, however, the most disastrous year in Italy's history. Virtually every centre of population became a battleground and Italian cities were left a scene of utter devastation. As the Germans were pushed north with their backs against the mountains, some of the bitterest and bloodiest fighting of all took place in the Po Valley, fought by the partisans, who were about to overrun the area when the Allies finally arrived in April 1945. (The bitter fighting for control of the Po Valley is dramatised with newsreel clarity in Roberto Rossellini's film *Paisa* made in 1946.) When a partisan was captured nothing less than a summary death sentence could be expected and the Germans were not averse to carrying these out in public. On one occasion, partisans were executed by firing squad outside Teatro Coccia and, in their memory, the square along one side of which the Coccia stands was renamed Piazza Martiri della Libertá. The names of all those men and women of Novara who gave their lives are recorded on marble tablets set into the courtyard wall of the Broletto.

Cantelli gave a concert at Teatro Coccia during the 1944 season and another in January 1945. Shortly after this, he moved to Vercelli for a last concentrated operatic season. Between January and March, performances were given of *Tosca, Madama Butterfly* and *Rigoletto*. Apart from two performances of *La traviata* in October that year, these were the last standard repertory operas that Guido Cantelli directed from the orchestra pit until *Così fan tutte* at Piccola Scala in 1956.

Cantelli now began to reveal more of himself to friends, always preferring a small intimate group in whom he could confide with safety to a wide circle of acquaintances whose idea of friendship was a desire to be seen with the right person. As Cantelli's fame increased, these "hangers-on" induced in him a sense of disgust. This accounts for the often-expressed opinion that Cantelli was a "cold" man with little or no humour. Both Folco Perrino and Giuseppe Gallini were able to refute this. On his own admission, Giuseppe Gallini was probably Cantelli's closest friend, especially in the important years between 1948 and 1952, when he was building his international career. The Cantelli he knew: " . . . never laughed when he was conducting, outside the theatre he was a very amusing man who liked to joke. Not with anybody, only with people he loved. He was a very polite, rather shy man." Folco Perrino experienced very similiar feelings: "He was a very slender man, but looked very florid. His features — beautiful hands — full of spirituality. A very aristocratic and very reserved man — meditative. He was very close to his *fiancè*, they were always together."

During that season in Vercelli, Guido and Iris decided to marry. They knew they had the blessing of Antonio and Angela and felt that her parents would just have to become reconciled to this logical outcome of their relationship. Their marriage took place on April 28, 1945, one day after Guido's twenty-fifth birthday. Msgr. Leone Ossola, Bishop of Novara, solemnised their wedding in his private chapel attached to the Cathedral of Novara. Lack of transport prevented Ghedini and his wife arriving from Turin to act as principal witnesses. Instead bride and groom were attended by partisan friends, unshaven and shabbily dressed, who deposited their rifles among the holy vestments on entering the chapel. At the end of the ceremony these were retrieved and a bizarre guard of honour mounted as the partisans accompanied Guido and Iris

Iris Bilucaglia

Guido Cantelli

annunciano il loro matrimonio

Novara, 28 aprile 1945

Novara
Massimo d'Azeglio, 9

An invitation card to Iris and Guido's wedding. Reproduced by courtesy of Mariangela Cantelli.

through Novara's deserted streets for a wedding breakfast at her parents' apartment.

That same day, April 28, Colonel Valerio (real name Walter Audisio) arrived at the farmhouse on Lake Como where Mussolini was being kept under arrest, ostensibly to take him back to Milan. After Mussolini and his mistress Claretta Petacci had driven one mile in Valerio's car they were taken out and shot and their bodies strung upside down at a petrol station on Milan's Piazzale Loreto. Partisans liberated Milan the following day.

*

As Italy rejoiced, the liberation became Guido and Iris's honeymoon. Realising that Guido would be better placed to develop his career in Milan the Cantellis rented a tiny apartment at Via Livorno 5, effectively their only home throughout their years together. Later as rooms emptied and money came in from conducting engagements they were able to rent more space until they occupied a couple of floors. Via Livorno stands two minutes walk away from Milan Conservatory, and is a miniscule street looking in 1978 much as it must have when Guido and Iris first moved there. Number five, however, was demolished some time in the Sixties, to be replaced by a tasteful modern apartment block, and all that remains is a portion of the garden at the rear.

For Iris, it was a time of readjustment, as previously she had not come into contact with the daily household chores, these being taken care of by her parent's maid. Happy as the couple were to be together they could not conceal the fact they they were desperately short of money. On many occasions their only full meal of the day came through the generosity of their neighbours. Even a small sum of money held in trust by Iris's parents only brought a temporary measure of relief. Any spare cash available went to buy scores and, as Guido now lived a short distance from Gallini's, he became an even more frequent customer. Giuseppe Gallini is convinced that Cantelli made great personal sacrifices in those post-war years, often deliberately going without meals, so that the money saved could be put towards the cost of a score he particularly wanted to study.

"He was very fluent in musical reading . . ." Giuseppe Gallini recalled, and went on to explain: "for instance, he was able to read a score he had never seen before, just sitting at the piano with the orchestral score, reading without interruption from beginning to end — sometimes even in our shop! He was able to read scores like someone else could read a newspaper." An analogy with books was suggested by Iris Cantelli, in Guido's process for selecting works that would enter his repertoire: "When you have read 1,000 books, you say this I prefer, and maybe you try to read that once again, so for the music it's the same." Guido Cantelli literally devoured scores.

Often, in those early Milan years, there would be lengthy periods between engagements which Guido spent at Via Livorno immersed in scores. Some were just perused, others prepared for the eventuality of a performance. How long this process took can be judged by Iris Cantelli's recollection of the time Guido devoted to an American composition that he included in one of his concerts with the NBC Symphony Orchestra: "For a modern score it was more difficult than an older score, because the rhythm is completely different. I think for a score of Don Gillis [Prairie Sunset — Portrait of a Frontier Town], it was a few minutes — possibly ten or twelve — three or four days were enough to know the score by memory."

This work only came under Cantelli's baton once, and in all probability he did not see the score until his arrival in America, so this is an extreme demonstration of his powers of concentration. Study of repertory works took far longer and once committed to memory would be re-studied constantly. For Guido Cantelli it was never a case of learning a work by heart then filing it away not to be looked at until an envisaged performance. Only by this constant re-studying, could Cantelli acheive complete identification with the composer's thoughts: for him, nothing less would do. These studies were made from miniature scores and Guido never collected biographical or reference books on the composers he conducted: for him whatever a composer had to say lay in the notes he had written, and it was the conductor's duty to study these, and get as close as he could to the truth contained therein.

*

When Dr. Antonio Ghiringhelli became Superintendant of Teatro alla Scala in May 1945 he inherited a theatre in ruins. On August 15, 1943, the RAF had launched a massive bombing raid over Milan, and La Scala received a direct hit, leaving only a shell consisting of four walls: walls on which during the occupation had been scrawled the words "Viva Toscanini" as a token of resistance. All that remained of La Scala's company was the orchestra, though it too had suffered the ravages of war and was hardly the instrument it had once been.

Dr. Ghiringhelli's first task was to organise a series of open air concerts, featuring the Scala orchestra, in the courtyard of Milan's Castello Sforzesco. During the twenty-seven years that Dr. Ghiringhelli worked at La Scala, it was his policy to encourage young artists and these concerts enabled him to put that ideal into practice. Consultation took place between Dr. Ghiringhelli and Riccardo Pick-Mangiagalli, Director of Milan Conservatory, with a view to inviting some recently graduated students to take part in the series. On a long term basis, Ghiringhelli had in mind a plan whereby a close association would be formed between the Conservatory and La Scala, giving outstanding students regular opportunities to perform in the theatre. From these original talks, Pick-Mangiagalli put forward his outstanding pianist — Marcello Abbado, and outstanding conductor — Guido Cantelli.

Other forces were lobbying for Cantelli too. Antonino Votto saw these concerts as an important opportunity for his one time pupil. Clement Petrillo, now Dean of Philadelphia College of the Performing Arts, described how Maestro Votto approached him on Cantelli's behalf:

> During my tenure in Milano and La Scala during the war, as officer in charge of the Opera and Concerts Office for Allied Military Government, Maestro Antonio Votto . . . approached me about Guido Cantelli. He praised Cantelli's talent and as I recall, asked if he could be given the opportunity to conduct La Scala orchestra. I took this up with the committee administering La Scala with me at the time. All agreed to have Mr. Cantelli conduct the orchestra at the outdoor concerts at Castello Sforzesco . . .

When at last the final arrangements were completed and made public, the news that young musicians were involved did not fall as sweet music on the ears of certain members of La Scala's orchestra. A representative went to see Dr. Ghiringhelli saying that they did not want "young musicians" as, to them it would be akin to "throwing Daniel to the Lions!"

Hours and hours of work by Cantelli went into putting the programme together, with the final selection resulting from any number of rejected possibilites. Weber's overture *Ruler of the Spirits* opened the concert which took place on July 27, 1945. Tchaikovsky's Sixth followed and, after the interval, Marcello Abbado performed *Humoresque* for piano and orchestra by Pick-Mangiagalli, which despite its diminutive title contains a bravura piano part, reflecting Pick-Mangiagalli's own prowess on the instrument.

Marcello Abbado now occupies the position once held by Pick-Mangiagalli, and he remembers what it felt like at rehearsals prior to the concert: "The atmosphere was of great enthusiasm. Above all Cantelli was very happy to conduct such an orchestra. He wanted perfection, so he was intent to try and get from the orchestra the most possible. There was a great amount of affection for this young musician, they all admired this young conductor."

Whatever doubts members of the orchestra might have expressed beforehand about Cantelli's abilities, once he was on the podium they recognised his potential, even though in his quest for perfection Cantelli kept stopping the orchestra every few bars to explain what he required. It was a discipline the musicians of La Scala's orchestra had not encountered before, and was least expected from one so young, so Cantelli's success speaks eloquently of his power, even at that age, to mould an orchestra of hard-bitten professionals to his will.

Two short pieces concluded the programme, *The Swan of Tuonela* by Sibelius and Rossini's overture *Le siège de Corinthe*. The vast audience in the courtyard greeted Cantelli's interpretations with tremendous acclaim, later Tabanelli, the orchestra's tympanist, voiced the opinion of his fellow musicians when he reported to the committee managing La Scala that the orchestra had been "enthralled" by Cantelli's conducting. "It was not the most important musical event [in Milan after the war], but the birth of a great conductor." (Marcello Abbado)

*

Five days later, an offer to conduct a broadcast concert, to be transmitted on August 19, was received from Italian radio (RAI). With so little time, Guido did not feel able to prepare a new programme so he suggested a repeat of the Tchaikovsky Sixth. This performance, in which he conducted RAI's own symphony orchestra at their concert hall in Turin, was broadcast nationwide and brought his name to a far wider audience, resulting in invitations being extended for engagements that in the following three years were to take Cantelli all over Italy.

*

The Maino family sponsored a series of family, musical evenings at their house on the outskirts of Milan during the spring of 1946. Over several months, a wide variety of music received performances by instrumental groups, chamber orchestras, quartets and soloists — Arturo Benedetti Michelangeli among them. Cantelli directed three concerts for the Maino family and was a regular member of the audience. As Milan was still under military curfew, these "evenings" usually ran through till morning. Inevitably, La Scala and its phoenix-like resurrection from the pile of rubble was a topic of conversation. Money for the reconstruction came from the allied military governments, donations from troops stationed in Italy and a gift of one million lire from Toscanini. A rumour was circulating that Toscanini would be returning to Italy, and conducting at the re-opening of the theatre. Eventually this was confirmed with the announcement that he would be conducting the opening gala opera concert on May 11, with two more concerts to follow.

Toscanini's second concert was a particularly demanding orchestral programme, which he refused to change, despite Ghiringhelli's fears that the orchestra would not be up to it. There were five works in a virtuoso programme designed to tax any orchestra: Kabalevsky's Overture: *Colas Breugon*, Brahms' Third Symphony, Gershwin's *An American in Paris*, Respighi's *Fontane di Roma* and Debussy's *La mer*.

At Toscanini's request, young musicians were invited to attend the rehearsals for this concert and Cantelli received an invitation by way of the conservatory. There are suggestions that Cantelli may have actually been introduced to Toscanni during a rehearsal break but, if this is true, it was little more than a brief handshake. For Cantelli though, the rehearsal was a revelation sending him back to his scores, probing even further in search of a total command over every musical facet. Toscanini's powers of concentration and control stimulated Cantelli's studies to such an extent that he cancelled at least one engagement and would not rest content until his new ideals were attained. When an engagement did approach, Cantelli would abstain from alcohol and cigarettes demonstrating the seriousness and dedication of his approach.

August 1946 brought Cantelli to Rome for his first concert with the Orchestra del Accademia di Santa Cecilia during their summer season of open air programmes at the Basilica di Massenzio. Franco Ferrara, the conductor, was present at the rehearsals, and still remembers Cantelli's impact:

> In the rehearsal he was very fast, and I saw he was a very great talent. He was very mature when he started to conduct, very good musically and technically. The orchestra was quiet, that's important in Italy, because they talk during rehearsal and you see if they like the conductor when they don't speak. In the rehearsal of Cantelli, the orchestra was very quiet, they listened because what he did was very good. I remember well a performance of *La valse* by Ravel — a very difficult piece — then they saw how good was this young musician.

A debilitating illness, causing sudden fainting attacks, often during a performance, has severely curtailed Franco Ferrara's career. More than once Guido heard a Ferrara broadcast interrupted through this, yet he was deeply impressed by Ferrara's musicianship. This concert in Rome brought them together for a lifelong friendship. With Ferrara's public appearances becoming more and more infrequent, he has developed a secondary career as a teacher of conducting. This was many years after their first meeting but one wonders if Cantelli regarded the older and more experienced conductor as a teacher as well as a friend. "I had a great admiration for Cantelli," explained Franco Ferrara, "it was absolutely not contact between teacher and pupil — just of respect."

Guido's respect of a fellow musician, was brought into sharp juxtaposition at the Ninth Festival Internazionale di Musica Contemporanea, held in September at Teatro La Fenice, in Venice. Cantelli gave a concert that included a performance of Leonard Bernstein's *Jeremiah* Symphony. In the same programme, Ildebrando Pizzetti was leading a performance of his recent Violin Concerto. A managerial error booked two rehearsals for exactly the same time, and Cantelli was told he would have to make do with only a single rehearsal for an extremely complex programme. Cantelli refused to accept this and, after much argument, schedules were re-arranged and he was given a second rehearsal. Arriving at La Fenice for this, Guido was informed that he would have to cancel it, as Pizzetti at that very moment was stepping on to the podium for a run-through of his Violin Concerto. Angered, Cantelli rushed over to Pizzetti, telling him in no uncertain terms just what he thought of his action in usurping the rehearsal alloted to him. "You haven't any respect, even for a man of my age," Pizzetti replied to Guido's outburst. Looking Pizzetti coldly in the face Guido answered, "When confronted with my responsibility towards music, I could not even respect my own father!" After a violent scene involving everyone connected with the festival, Cantelli's powerful argument eventually led to his rehearsal being reinstated.

Cantelli would not tolerate half measures where the interpretation of a piece of music was concerned. He expected concert managements and orchestras to provide all the facilities requisite for bringing any given work to concert pitch. Contemporary works acted as a tempering of Guido's natural inclination towards romantic music. "He realised in the first years of conducting, that he was too romantic, because he chose at once Tchaikovsky. The moment he realised that, he tried to learn and study some scores less romantic — but it was difficult for him." (Iris Cantelli).

There is an irony here, as shortly in these pages Guido Cantelli will be described as a "modern and contemporary conductor." Whether Cantelli directed old music, or works straight from the composer's pen, as he did on several occasions, his approach was always the same: "He never thought, 'I'm a pioneer.' He would say, 'This is the music that I love, and I want the people that come to the concert to love it too.'" (Iris Cantelli)

It was a philosophy that applied equally to every piece of music that Guido Cantelli touched.

When he directed the Maggio Musicale Fiorentino at Florence, Cantelli made his first acquaintance with an orchestra, to which he would return for a brief intense association. The concert in Florence was given on November 24, 1946: exactly a decade of music-making lay ahead of him.

*

ENSA — or to use its full title, Entertainment National Service Association — were responsible for providing entertainment for the British forces stationed in Italy. Many of these troops remained behind after the liberation assisting in the massive task of reconstruction. An entirely new situation regarding forces entertainment now prevailed and in 1946 ENSA was closed down and replaced by a new organization, Combined Services Entertainment, managed by the army.

The officer commanding Combined Services Entertainment was Major Arthur Watson, whose responsibility for live entertainment and film presentations covered the Italian peninsula and Austria. His first project was the requisitioning of opera houses, with the intention of mounting performances. Most were in a terrible condition with vital stage machinery absent, seats ripped out and structural damage often beyond repair. Major Watson's teams did what they could to put the theatres into some form of working order and the earliest performances given under these circumstances were strictly for the troops, who paid a nominal entrance fee. Later the performances were opened to the local people as well.

As word got around, Major Watson soon found himself well supplied with artists, as singers, dancers and musicians freely offered their services. Indeed, the concerts were so successful that, in April 1947, Major Watson was requested by army headquarters to arrange a tour by the Florence Symphony Orchestra. It was suggested that he should engage two or more "celebrated" conductors, and he automatically chose Victor de Sabata, but finding another proved to be something of a problem. Arthur Watson recalled how this was resolved:

> The harpist of the Florence Symphony suggested I might get in touch with a new young Italian conductor by the name of Guido Cantelli. So I telephoned the leading concert agency in Rome, Signorina Camus [Clara], she was the director, and we met. She said, 'Guido Cantelli arrives this morning at twelve o'clock in Rome, and I'll introduce you to him.'
>
> I met him, then we had dinner that evening; we arranged his fee, and he agreed to do the concerts. He particularly asked what kind of tastes the young soldiers had. I said normally the popular classics — Beethoven, Tchaikovsky, etc. He had not got a great repertoire of classics then, he was

more of a modern and contemporary conductor. He said, 'I know Beethoven's Eighth' — which he did.

Guido's programme also included the Mendelssohn Violin Concerto, performed by the orchestra's leader. The concerts were given twice at each venue, and these were: Padova, Udine, Trieste and Venice. Because of the conditions under which they worked, each conductor played only one programme, time not being available for the extra rehearsals needed to include any additional works.

Combined Services Entertainment had requisitioned or specially taken over for the concerts all the theatres in which the performances were given, and had even arranged for hotels normally occupied by visiting British artists to accommodate the musicians.

Victor de Sabata was in the end not available to undertake the tour, so Cantelli shared the podium with Igor Markevitch. Markevitch had spent the war years in Italy and at the end of the war was appointed principal conductor of the Maggio Musicale Fiorentino — Arthur Watson's Florence Symphony Orchestra. He was able to observe Cantelli at work with the orchestra, and he too looked upon him as a conductor of modern works, with a limited number of compositions from the standard repertoire. Markevitch had no hesitation in offering Cantelli advice:

> I remember also to have recommended to him often to acquire a much wider repertory, telling him that it was essential to be able to present the whole of the musical literature and not to choose only a few programmes from it to present himself.

> My relationship with Guido was very good although he was rather closed up and of a reserved nature. I would say even that he was in fact an introverted person. However, he took confidence in me when he saw that I sincerely wanted to help him, and he gladly accepted my advice, especially for the Eighth Symphony by Beethoven which was on his programme and which he played a little too much in the Italian manner . . .

In Franco Ferrara's opinion this is a highly contentious statement: "That's a very dangerous thing to speak about. I don't believe in an Italian kind of interpretation for Beethoven, the important thing in a performance is that it convinces. And that was so with Cantelli, and so I don't accept this discussion about an Italian kind of interpretation of Beethoven."

There was also some practical assistance from Markevitch: he gave Cantelli one of his batons, as those he used were not really very good. Later it became a source of great pride for Guido to explain that his batons were made for him by the man who made Toscanini's.

Trieste . 7. 4 .47

Eg.° Major Watson

Ho ricevuto a Milano il telegramma
ma poco prima della mia partenza per
Trieste. Accetto di dirigere i 6 concerti
fermo restando il contratto già firmato
per 229.000 Lire. Come Lei saprà 22 mila
dovrò versarle alla Signorina Comus.

Avrò il piacere di vederla qui a Trieste
per il mio concerto del 10?

Le ricambio le mie più vive
cordialità

Guido. Cantelli

*Guido's contract and letter of acceptance. Reproduced by courtesy of Arthur
Watson.*

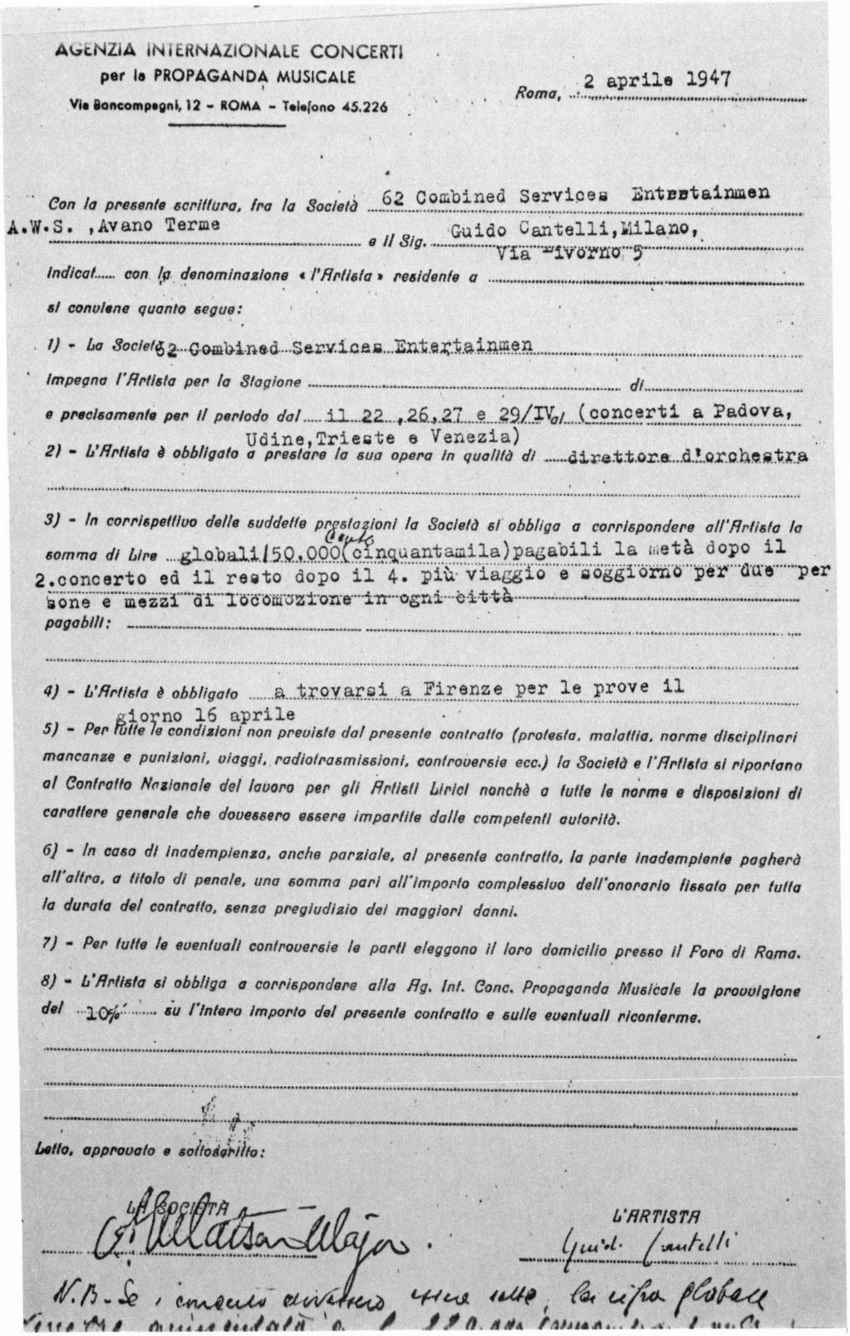

AGENZIA INTERNAZIONALE CONCERTI
per la PROPAGANDA MUSICALE
Via Boncompagni, 12 – ROMA – Telefono 45.226

Roma, 2 aprile 1947

Con la presente scrittura, fra la Società 62 Combined Services Entertainmen A.W.S. ,Avano Terme *e il Sig.* Guido Cantelli,Milano, *indicat...... con la denominazione « l'Artista » residente a* Via Livorno 5

si conviene quanto segue:

1) – La Società 62 Combined Services Entertainmen *impegna l'Artista per la Stagione .... di .... e precisamente per il periodo dal* il 22 ,26,27 e 29/IV *al* (concerti a Padova, Udine,Trieste e Venezia)

2) – L'Artista è obbligato a prestare la sua opera in qualità di direttore d'orchestra

3) – In corrispettivo delle suddette prestazioni la Società si obbliga a corrispondere all'Artista la somma di Lire globali 150.000(cinquantamila)pagabili la metà dopo il 2.concerto ed il resto dopo il 4. più viaggio e soggiorno per due persone e mezzi di locomozione in ogni città
pagabili:

4) – L'Artista è obbligato a trovarsi a Firenze per le prove il giorno 16 aprile

5) – Per tutte le condizioni non previste dal presente contratto (protesta, malattia, norme disciplinari mancanze e punizioni, viaggi, radiotrasmissioni, controversie ecc.) la Società e l'Artista si riportano al Contratto Nazionale del lavoro per gli Artisti Lirici nonchè a tutte le norme e disposizioni di carattere generale che dovessero essere impartite dalle competenti autorità.

6) – In caso di inadempienza, anche parziale, al presente contratto, la parte inadempiente pagherà all'altra, a titolo di penale, una somma pari all'importo complessivo dell'onorario fissato per tutta la durata del contratto, senza pregiudizio dei maggiori danni.

7) – Per tutte le eventuali controversie le parti eleggono il loro domicilio presso il Foro di Roma.

8) – L'Artista si obbliga a corrispondere alla Ag. Int. Conc. Propaganda Musicale la provvigione del 10% *su l'intero importo del presente contratto e sulle eventuali riconferme.*

Letto, approvato e sottoscritto:

LA SOCIETÀ [illegible] L'ARTISTA Guido Cantelli

N.B. – Se i concerti avvenissero [illegible] la cifra globale
[illegible] 220.000 [illegible]

At each concert Cantelli received a standing ovation from the troops and he delighted in signing autographs for them. From the start it had been obvious that he was building up a tremendous rapport with the orchestra. According to Arthur Watson; "they worshipped him — he was one of them!" When it finally came to an end a party was thrown in a hotel at Padova; maybe it evoked a memory of his spell in the jazz band, as Guido found himself seated at the piano, generally helping things to go with a swing! As they were all going their separate ways, Guido approached Major Watson with a proposition:

> He was very enthusiastic about his reception with the Allied troops, and he must have appreciated the reactions of the British troops in particular, because he said, 'Can you get me some work in London?' I did try, I wrote to S.A. Gorlinsky, who at that time was running concerts for Jack Hylton — I think they were taking place at one of the huge auditoria like Wembley [Stadium] — but I was too late, as the programmes had already been arranged. In other words, Gorlinsky had signed up his conductors . . .

S.A. Gorlinsky would later become Cantelli's agent and impresario in London promoting all his concerts with the Philharmonia Orchestra; but, in April 1947, regular seasons in London were still four years away.

*

"Franco, I'm afraid in Vienna for the first time," Guido wrote to Franco Mannino, apprehensive at his first appearance outside Italy, with the Vienna Symphony Orchestra, on April 28, 1948, at which Mannino was to play Tchaikovsky's First Piano Concerto.

"Very precious," was how Franco Mannino described his memories of Guido Cantelli, whom he remembered introducing himself after a concert performance in Milan, around 1945. His friendship too lasted unbroken, despite a brief lapse; and Mannino's later career has encompassed both composing and conducting — he was musical director on the last films of Luchino Visconti. Whilst Guido had poured out his anxieties by letter, once involved in the music — as Mannino soon learnt —Guido had very specific ideas about how to perform the concerto:

> My experience with Guido is wonderful, because Guido was a very good musician and also a very good conductor. However . . . when he heard your musical opinion of a work — NO CHANGE! — and this is very difficult for soloists . . . he was very intransigent. He was right for the music — would make no compromises, and sometimes he seemed strong with you, but he was very human.

Cantelli, billed in the programme as hailing from Rome, had in Franco Mannino's words, "a tremendous success." It was the only occasion Cantelli appeared in Vienna which at that period was still a divided city with Russian, French, British and American sectors. Cantelli and Mannino were sharing a room in a hotel in the Russian sector and, on their return from the concert a post-mortem lasting several hours took place. A remark by Cantelli has remained imprinted on Franco Mannino's memory: "He was sure that his career would be very important, in a short time."

During the night they both awoke in a cold sweat, as heavy footsteps could be heard drawing closer and closer, amplified by the hotel's echoing corridor. Terrified, they listened and watched as the footsteps ceased and their bedroom door opened casting a huge shadow on the wall. Reaching a climax worthy of Alfred Hitchcock, for its combination of terror and humour, it turned out to be the night porter coming to see if they wanted their shoes polished!

*

Away from music, Cantelli's overriding passion was football. Introduced to the game by his father, who served on the committee of Novara Football Club, Cantelli never wavered in his support for the home team. These were the years when Novara were constantly heading league tables and winning through to championship finals. As Guido spent more and more time away from Italy he arranged for the results of these vital matches to be transmitted to wherever he was currently engaged. During a season in New York Walter Toscanini cabled a winning result, which delighted Guido no end and he pinned the telegram on the bathroom wall, as a reminder of his team's good fortune. With his increasing fame, and Novara becoming known as his birthplace through programme biographies, the team officials often invited their most celebrated supporter to watch the match from their box. Cantelli, although grateful to be asked, always declined, feeling that his place was on his own "spot" on the terraces, shouting encouragement and surrounded by fellow supporters. This devotion to Novara would take Cantelli anywhere: once when they were playing an away match he phoned Giuseppe Gallini — not a great football enthusiast — to see if he could drive him to the match, Giuseppe agreed — and found himself driving 500 miles!

When the results were broadcast on Sunday evenings, Guido listened with an ear normally reserved for a work of music, each score being entered in the score check printed in "Gazzetta dello Sport." This was the only newspaper he bought, and each weekly edition was read cover to cover. Cantelli preferred to read about sport; critical writings on his performances did not interest him. After an early performance with the NBC Symphony Orchestra he was appalled to read that his interpretation was the finest heard by that critic in a decade. How, he thought, could his youthful interpretation be considered greater than that of Toscanini, who had performed that very same work for the NBC only months before?

Cars were the other great passion of Cantelli's life. The faster the car, the more Guido appreciated its qualities. As each lost its fascination, another would be purchased in exchange, culminating in his last and proudest possession a Ferrari. In the "Scotsman" interview, quoted earlier, Guido had this to say about cars: ". . . it is not that I just love speed, but a car for me is something participating in my enthusiasm. I need a car that will go fast and will really answer all my demands." To this end, Guido was a frequent spectator at Monza, acquiring a motor racing driver's licence and taking lessons from the famous driver Taruffi.

*

Cantelli directed two concerts at Teatro La Fenice at the beginning of April 1948. Wandering into La Fenice, he found Franco Ferrara recording Nino Rota's score for the film *The Glass Mountain*. The climax of the film is a sub-Puccini operatic scene taken from an opera entitled *The Legend of the Glass Mountain*, composed by the hero Richard Wilder (Michael Denison) and featuring Tito Gobbi. Cantelli watched avidly whilst the score was pre-recorded by Gobbi, accompanied by La Fenice's orchestra and chorus, under Ferrara. Between sessions, the three musicians sat in St. Mark's square at a pavement cafe, and in one break went to the cinema to see Walt Disney's *Bambi*, which Franco Ferrara remembered them watching as "three adults in a cinema full of children!"

*

As each post war NBC Symphony season closed, Toscanini returned to Italy for a vacation, divided between his house on Milan's Via Durini and a retreat on Isolino di San Giovanni, the island on Lake Maggiore. Arriving in 1948, Toscanini informed Dr. Ghiringhelli that he was looking for an assistant to work with him and the NBC Symphony Orchestra, and asked him if he could recommend any possible candidates. Dr. Ghiringhelli recalled that he had had two possible conductors in mind: but not Cantelli.

On May 21, Toscanini attended a concert at La Scala, joining Dr. Ghiringhelli in box fourteen. During the programme, Toscanini suddenly grabbed Ghiringhelli's arm saying in an excited whisper: "that is me directing this concert." He saw in the twenty-eight year old Guido Cantelli, making his debut at Teatro alla Scala, a reflection of his own musical personality at the beginning of his career. This revelation came as a total surprise on Toscanini, the concert being his first encounter with Cantelli's conducting. Dr. Ghiringhelli is quite emphatic that Toscanini was not present at the rehearsals and that his excitement stemmed purely from hearing Cantelli conduct the orchestra in concert. Thirty years have surrounded this crucial incident in Cantelli's life with all manner of theatrical accretions, in view of this and Dr. Ghiringhelli's utter contradiction, the question was put to him again (through an interpreter): "Was Toscanini present at Cantelli's rehearsals?" Emphatically he repeated: "Toscanini was not present at Cantelli's rehearsals."

Cantelli's programme for the concert on May 21 contained the following works:

Ravel: *Rhapsodie Espagnole*
Brahms: Violin Concerto (with Nathan Milstein)
Busoni: *Berceuse élégiaque*
Hindemith: *Mathis der Maler* Symphony

Looked at objectively, Cantelli's career from the concert at Castello Sforzesco was that of a journeyman conductor, taking a route almost predestined to bring about a conjunction with Toscanini. It's as though Cantelli's entire life had been a progression leading up to this moment.

A few days later, Guido received a formal invitation from Toscanini to direct the NBC Symphony Orchestra in four concerts the following January and February. At the same time, wishing to get to know Guido away from a musical environment, Toscanini invited himself for an afternoon at Via Livorno. With him he brought his latest recording, newly arrived from America, awaiting his approval for publication — and auditioned it on Guido's radiogram.

WITH TOSCANINI

On September 11 and 12, Cantelli directed a triple bill: *L'Incubo* (*The Nightmare*) by the Italian, Riccardo Nielsen, *Les malheurs d'Orphée* by Milhaud and *The Telephone* by Menotti, at the eleventh Festival Internazionale di Musica Contemporanea, held at Teatro La Fenice. From Venice, Cantelli journeyed by train to Siena for a concert devoted to the Venetian, Baldassare Galuppi (1706–1785), at one time director of music at St. Mark's. This concert was promoted by L'Accademia Chigiana as part of their annual festival of baroque music and given on September 22. The next day, Cantelli was due to perform a programme of choral and orchestral music by Cavalli (1602–1676) in Perugia, for the Sagra Musicale Umbra, whose festival features compositions of all periods relating to a liturgical theme. Whilst in Venice, Guido had to some extent fought off an attack of bronchitis but it surfaced again during the rehearsal at Perugia. Arriving to find the orchestra and chorus ill-prepared, and with very little rehearsal time available, Guido felt sharp pangs of musical frustration gnawing at him, and was tempted to give up and take time off to rid himself of the bronchitis. Despite generous offers by the management to postpone the concert until he felt satisfied with the results Cantelli simply walked out and returned to Milan.

October and November brought the remaining engagements of the year at Brussels and Palermo. Throughout, not unnaturally, Cantelli's thoughts were becoming focussed on America and the preparation of his four concerts with the NBC Symphony. Such was the state of the Cantellis' finances that Guido would have to travel alone as only enough money for one passage could be raised. Giuseppe Gallini drove him to Genoa, the port of departure. Thinking back, Gallini recalled that whatever emotions were running through Cantelli at that moment were kept perfectly under control: "I was surprised because Guido was completely unexcited, very quiet without any particular tension, and he was not nervous. Before he left, Guido has studied as he has never studied before, aware that he was going to face one of the best and most difficult orchestras in the world. In spite of that he was completely quiet, that in my opinion is a very good test of the real structure of his character."

The S.S. Vulcania, with Cantelli aboard, sailed from Genoa on

December 17. Just prior to embarking a telegram arrived from Toscanini:

With my kindest wishes for a good crossing. Goodbye till soon.

Arturo Toscanini

*

Throughout Guido's sojourn in America, he wrote Iris a long series of letters — here published in English for the first time. These vividly describe his work with the NBC Symphony Orchestra, and the artistic agonies he endured to secure the performances he required. At the same time, Cantelli was swept into the social ambience surrounding Toscanini, who is always referred to as "The Maestro." All this finds expression in the letters, but little is said about his feelings towards America. Immersed in music, America passed Cantelli by on this occasion, although later visits were to produce a more positive reaction! However, Guido's first meeting with the "New World" appeared to bode well for the future:

I arrived at nine o' clock in the morning [it was December 30], and Walter [Toscanini] and two men from the NBC were waiting for me. The business with the customs was to be long, but in less than half an hour we came out of the door, and I was first. The car of the Maestro was waiting, and carried me quickly to the NBC. Here I received a telephone call from the Maestro, who was even more affectionate with me.

We went to my hotel to leave the luggage, and then to Riverdale [Toscanini's New York home], to eat in his house. A dream . . .

In the afternoon with the Maestro again at the NBC, in order to be present at the rehearsal of Ansermet. He was rehearsing Bartók's, *Music for Strings, Percussion and Celestà*, the orchestra was first class, simply superb!

Guido then sums up his thoughts on looking back at the year now drawing to its close:

. . . 1948 was certainly very good for me, almost undescribable. . . in 1949, I will have to go towards it, and I will try to do it with all my strength, and above all with the whole of myself.

For the moment he could relax. Toscanini had arranged a New Year's eve party, for about fifty people. Guido shared a table with Ansermet and his wife, but not for long, as the room was made ready for a *divertissement*:

. . . there was a small performance by [Samuel] Chotzinoff [The General Music Director of NBC, and the Manager of the NBC Symphony Orchestra], Wanda Horowitz and many other friends. There was even Milstein who played in a fey way . . . A parody of the Valkyries with Chotzinoff, who sang in German, was extremely good. He was dressed in an indescribable manner and Wanda was playing the part of Sieglinde. And there were so many other small scenes. The Maestro and myself sat in the front row!

Festivities continued the following evening at the house of Lucrezia Bori, who had been a leading soprano with Toscanini during his years as musical director of the Metropolitan company before the First World War. She obviously made an impression on Cantelli, as his letter continues:

... without wanting to, I complimented my host, which had a tremendous success. Lucrezia Bori has in reality passed sixty years, but if you were to see her, with her figure, you wouldn't say she was more than forty!

Music was never far from Guido's mind, and his next letter begins:

I studied all morning, then went to eat with the famous baritone, [Giuseppe] de Luca and his wife — friends of the Maestro. They live in the same hotel as me. With us was the Signorina [Margherita] de Vecchi — don't get agitated, Walter calls her the 'Statue of Liberty!' She is ten years younger than the Maestro. She knows everyone and knows everything. She is the daughter of a very well-known Piedmont doctor, who at an early age went to live in California and is, above all, one of the most influential persons of the Italian community. But everything that she does is because of her grand admiration for Toscanini.

Later she accompanied me to Carnegie Hall, for a concert given by the Philharmonic [New York Philharmonic Symphony] conducted by Charles Munch, and that orchestra made a terrific impression on me. When going out Margherita de Vecci presented me to Bruno Zirato, a man of Calabria — but all he could remember of his country are the sunsets! He's the manager of the Philharmonic, and a good friend of the Maestro's. He said that a few evenings ago, while eating with Toscanini, there was a lot of talk about me and, imitating Toscanini in his gestures he repeated to me, 'He mustn't imitate me, he must be himself, I hope he'll do it for me.' And that is what you have always told me, and I swear to you — as I swear to the Maestro — that I will make you happy in that respect.

Now I'm going to bed, I'm tired. I've studied a lot. Tomorrow I'm going to study at the NBC, in the Maestro's dressing room — you will understand what sort of study it is!

I can't give you my impressions of New York, I barely know it at all. These days I am trying not to distract myself, because the serious days are approaching. I feel that they are expecting me; they continue to photograph me . . .

I myself am only thinking about my great battle, if it goes well the game will be won. A game however, because it doesn't seem possible that I have arrived in so short a time, at so much. In order to understand the importance of this position, you really need to be here.

Guido then writes about his first session with Toscanini:

I've been the whole day at the NBC, and in the afternoon together with the Maestro, listening to the rehearsals of Ansermet. When it was over, we went back to the studio and discussed the Haydn symphony. I let him see my score, and he found some notes that I had made to be quite justified. At one point I made, saying there should be a crescendo which wasn't written, he was really enthusiastic and gave me the most beautiful of smiles, and embraced me saying, 'Go on, what good sense you have, and how you know what you want.'

After the session, there followed an incident which more than any musical example draws attention to the way Toscanini's relationship with Cantelli was developing. As Guido explains:

In the corner of the studio was the Signora Cia, the wife of Walter. She took my overcoat (that heavy one), but the Maestro wanted to help me with it. You can imagine the scene, me first of all refusing, then deciding to allow him to, and I swear tears came to my eyes! Even those present remained impressed, with that gesture he was submitting himself and thanking me for the satisfaction I had given him.

I felt myself to be the most fortunate man of this world; I've got you — and him, the most and best friend that I will ever have, and he is Toscanini! I will do my best to make him happy.

I spent a delicious session in the studio of the Maestro, playing and discussing a lot. I swear to you, at each meeting I realise how much this man likes me. You can be sure, that if I was not able to satisfy him, I would bury myself underground.

There was still more socializing to be done, plus a promise to Iris:

Today we are at the Harknesses. What beautiful things I have seen, and what pictures: Picasso, Degas, Modigliani, Manet, Rouault ... At half-past two we went to another town, where Horowitz was giving a recital. As I didn't speak at the end of the recital with the piano player, I don't know what to write. I can tell you one thing, it is the first time I have really heard the piano played — and that's enough!

Back at the [Harkness] house we ate. Also there were Samuel Barber, Gian Carlo Menotti and the Milsteins. The way they were looking at me, I feel that I have a morbid aspect. From tomorrow on and for the next month, I will not accept any more invitations. I will concentrate on my work, and try to give the very best of myself.

Guido had now arrived at the moment of his first rehearsal with the NBC Symphony Orchestra. He opens the next letter with a rhetorical question, "How well did it go?"

... the Maestro embraced me twice, once at the end in front of the whole orchestra, then again in the dressing room, in the most affectionate manner. Everybody is happy except me. I'll tell you: After my big speech, I could not express myself in English, and in French it's even worse; there are many in the orchestra who could understand me in Italian, naturally, but I did not know this then and what I wanted to say was turning over inside me (you know what the harmonies of Hindemith are like) — you can imagine my torment.

The orchestra is without doubt excellent, but is is impossible to go straight away into details and obtain truly everything one wants. You know the first rehearsal with a new orchestra is always an arduous problem — because of the acoustics or the arrangement of the players and so on. I am sure I will improve the situation as I go on — not that it has been a difficult problem. Now that I know that I can express myself in Italian, I've removed this obstacle that was paralysing me a bit, and I will work with all that I have in full serenity.

Walter Toscanini had composed a few words in English for Guido to introduce himself to the orchestra. Although Guido read the words fairly well — after being rehearsed by Walter — he could not understand them. When a member of the orchestra replied, all Guido really understood was his "thank you' at the end. As the rehearsal progressed, Guido felt the need to explain a particularly difficult point, but his lack of English prevented him from putting across exactly what he was trying to say. Remo Bolognini, one of the first violins, put Guido at ease when he explained that he could speak Italian because, "we've been with Toscanini for quite a few years, you will see, it'll work and we will understand." As Guido explained to Iris, they did.

The rehearsals continued, along with the letters:

I daily return from the rehearsal with the Maestro in his car . . . Today a rehearsal of *Mathis*, which was superb, and a discreet Haydn. [Cantelli's first NBC concert contained Haydn's Symphony No. 93 and Hindemith's *Mathis der Maler*.] I said discreet, because it is the first time I have conducted it. I was certainly not master of myself, but Toscanini was extremely happy — even with the Symphony!

In the interval they took a lot of photographs of us, the Maestro and me, and at the end there were reporters from the press waiting for interviews. [Toscanini] waited for it to finish before embracing me and telling me with the most beautiful smile I have ever seen — 'I seem to have produced a son.' My heart stopped beating, and I swear to you that today will be an unforgettable day . . . hooray, I'm mad with joy!!

Much editorial comment was made on the fact that Guido was twenty-eight, and Toscanini eighty-two. One of the articles on that "unforgettable" day appeared in "Time, The Weekly Newsmagazine", (January 24, 1949). Headlined "Like I Do" it presents a portrait of Cantelli as the (unnamed) "Time" journalist had witnessed him during the NBC Symphony rehearsal:

The Toscanini-trained musicians of the NBC Symphony Orchestra blinked, then stared: Was it Frank Sinatra? At first glance, the boyish-looking new guest conductor was a dead ringer for Frankie: wispy, wire-thin, sallow-cheeked and dark-haired. But when 28-year-old Guido Cantelli stepped to the podium and rapped his baton, the jokes stopped. By the time Guido had driven them through bar-by-bar rehearsals of Hindemith and Haydn without looking at a score — gesturing and singing *fa — sol — la — tis* to make up for his lack of English — musicians were murmuring about "terrific talent."

Cried one hoarse but happy observer — Arturo Toscanini — as he shuffled from his aisle-seat listening post in Studio 8H: "Now here is a conductor — a good conductor."

Arturo Toscanini had dug up many an obscure piece of Italian music, but this was the first time in many a year he had unearthed a new Italian conductor — one who "conducts like I do," which means with precision, drama, warmth and love . . .

Guido is delighted with his chance to work with the NBC Symphony, though still somewhat bashful about his performance. Said he last week: "With this orchestra, there is no impassable level. If I could only express myself in English, I think I could get more from them."

Broadcast nationwide over the NBC network, Cantelli's first concert took place on January 15. Curiously, it is not the concert Guido writes about in his next letter, more the events afterwards:

I will not fail to describe to you, at the distance of one day, the reactions to my first concert. Representatives of the New York Philharmonic, who had been present at the concert, telephoned the Maestro this morning to ask him to arrange a booking during the next season. Margherita de Vecchi has been receiving telephone calls concerning me all day.

So things have gone well, and to that I don't want to add anything else, because it is necessary to see how the other concerts will go.

Rehearsals now commenced for the second concert:

I must tell you about today's rehearsal. In the first part I did *Romeo and Juliet* [Tchaikovsky] and here I really believed I had all eyes on me, even those of the Maestro behind my back. Then I went on to *Paganiniana* by Casella. At half-past-four I rested and went quickly to the Maestro to hear his impressions about the Tchaikovsky — 'Good, very good.' I swear to you, I don't understand anything any more, because it seemed the opposite to me! Being the first time, I found myself in difficulty at certain moments: tomorrow, I will be more frank.

Oh! I forgot to tell you, that yesterday Ansermet was at the rehearsal, together with Toscanini, and the latter told me what Ansermet said about me. Just imagine, Toscanini came to me with a terrific smile, to explain the enthusiasm of Ansermet. One other thing, is that yesterday Bernstein telephoned me, tomorrow he will be coming to the rehearsal, and I have accepted to eat with him. When I told Toscanini he shouted: 'Let all the conductors of America come, let them come and they will learn something.' And I continue not to understand anything?

Guido could not understand the interest he was generating and was still not convinced that he was achieving all he wanted to say in his conducting. Toscanini's public approval however, was making it only natural for other conductors to want to see what Cantelli was all about. After spending the evening with Bernstein, Guido writes to Iris with more than a hint of caution:

He's very pleasant, and showed affection towards me, as if I was an old friend of his. Will he also be a friend in the future?

The letters continue:

The rehearsal today was incredibly demanding. It's a difficult programme and it can't possibly be presented with only three rehearsals. Naturally with that orchestra one can do very much, but time is my enemy, one has to be patient. I am, but I'm certain that tomorrow the concert will be good if I can master myself and feel secure.

You know that at concerts sometimes I manage to surpass myself, that is my reward for my conscientious preparation and my absolute calm and serenity from the moment I get on to the podium. The latter is a gift I am extremely glad to have.

Guido then comments on the results of his sessions with the reporters and photographers:

After the rehearsal they showed me two of the most important magazines in America, where there were photographs of the Maestro and myself. There were so many things about me in the articles they had printed, so many funny things which they made me say — but which naturally I hadn't said — but then this is America!

The second concert broadcast on January 22, contained besides the Tchaikovsky and Casella already mentioned, Ghedini's *Pezzo concertante*. Guido's comments are restricted to the former works:

Here I am, back from the concert. I think everything went well — even the Tchaikovsky! I interpreted it a little in my own way, although in rehearsals, I tried to follow the suggestions of the Maestro. I'll tell you about this when I return ... Casella went well, but it could be done better, the lack of rehearsal time prevented me from going deep into it. After Tchaikovsky, the public gave me an ovation which was immense, but this was not enough for me because I was not able to be alone with the Maestro after the concert and don't yet know his impression.

This morning I slept late, and after eating went to Carnegie Hall to see Stokowski, I said to see, and again to see — what a funny chap! Talking about something else: I ate with two splendid women whom I got to know at Toscanini's house: Anne Marie Lacloche and Lohrian Franchetti — niece of the composer. With us that evening also for a meal at the Ziratos ... were the Maestro and Margherita. It was a pleasant evening, during which we heard a long series of memories of the Maestro . . .

How is it possible to fill myself thus with him? Truly like two old friends. Then today he told me — and this is just for you — things about me, which if I were to repeat them, no one would believe! It is a strong phrase, but I can tell you, he's really mad about me — I can just imagine your laughter!

After spending a day with Toscanini at Riverdale, Guido confessed to Iris:

. . . the Maestro, I swear, is now treating me as if I were his son. I can assure you that having such admiration and affection from such a man fills me with pride and gives me the strength to carry on and do better.

Now I leave you to go to bed, it is not late but I have set my alarm for seven o'clock. I will study in the morning and in the afternoon at three o'clock, I'll start the third battle with Bartók.

In 1949, Bartók's *Concerto for Orchestra* was still a recent composition and one that did not endear itself to Toscanini. As Guido explained to Iris:

The Maestro told me today that, having heard the records of the work by Bartók (which has been recorded here in America) he was not able to understand it at all. With a terrific smile, he gave me a pat on the back and said: 'You try and help me understand it.' I will try.

Guido continues by relating his experiences at the first rehearsal of the Bartók:

Today in two-and-a-half hours I have rehearsed the whole of the Bartók; but tomorrow, I want to do really well. Bartók is very well known here but for the NBC Orchestra this is a first performance, and I assure you that they will never have heard it done as I will do it. It's not a presumption of mine, but only the full consciousness of having studied it well.

Today the orchestra was impressed by the way I explained the music and sung it to them. At one point, I had an outburst in the style of Toscanini — 'I've got the Toscanini's' — as the Maestro says, because of an error that was repeated — no one was paying attention at that moment. The orchestra is very happy with me, and I had this confirmed today — the only rehearsal at which the Maestro was not present. (He's rehearsing, in his studio, a singer for *Aida*, which he will be doing.) However, I think that the marvellous discipline I've got derives a lot from his presence. They played at rehearsal as they did at the concert, therefore I am happy today for having given a demonstration of my preparation. Tomorrow I will do better!

Confirming this, Guido tells Iris:

Today I've worked like mad, Bartók is very difficult for everyone, fortunately

I know him very well. At the end of the rehearsal, Toscanini assured me that
— he always follows the rehearsals with a score — everything was very clear.
He told me when returning in the car — he always goes with me to the hotel
— that nobody could ever have studied that piece in such a way and, naturally,
it could never be performed as well as tomorrow.

. . . I hope to succeed in giving a good performance, I want to dedicate
it to the memory of Bartók. Perhaps if he were still living, he would have
appreciated my interpretation.

I forgot to tell you, that even in the [Wagner] *Faust* overture the Maestro
was in agreement. I was much afraid of this piece, they have produced only
a short while ago his record which is a masterpiece, and what's more, he
knew that it was my first performance.

That both Bartók and Wagner were a success in the concert given
on January 29, can be judged from Guido's next letter:

Everyone was enthusiastic. If Bartók had been able to hear me I think he
would have been contented. [His son Peter, wanting to hear Cantelli's
interpretation, was present at one of the rehearsals.] I am so happy my dear
Iris. Chotzinoff embraced me continually while he was announcing the
invitation for next year. The Maestro, at the peak of happiness, said in a loud
voice to everyone, 'That's what's known as conducting!'

The critic of "Time" magazine wrote today that the performance of the
Faust overture by Wagner was superb — that's a blessing — I wasn't at all
happy with it. In a long article he said that I have, 'the heart of a volcano'
and 'a brain of ice.' [These words actually appeared in the "New York
Times," on January 30.] The only criticism was about the length of the
intervals between the movements in Bartók. I got an invitation to increase
them in length, given that we had to fill fifty-five minutes.

Every day I am with the Maestro, who I adore. Tomorrow the final
battle will start. It will no longer be a question of saying better than that in
fact, I myself, would not have believed to win. I think always with each
concert, I must get better. I leave with the same fervour, the same sense of
responsibility as before.

In his final NBC concert, Guido included the Symphony in D minor
by Franck. On the surface a simple work, it is notoriously difficult to
bring off in performance with its subtle changes of tempo and broad
melodic spans. Guido thought it would be an easy work to rehearse,
expecting to spend an hour on it. Instead he worked on the first two
movements for over two-and-a-half hours. As he told Iris:

. . . so many things had to be said. The orchestra listened to me and played
with its whole heart, with all the passion I wanted.

Ravel's *La valse* completed the programme given on February 5.
"A magnificent concert, very enthusiastic, I can't think of anything better

to say than that," Guido wrote to Iris, but of course there was more to say:

The hall was completely full, they had added an extra 150 seats and even benches. Iris, I'm so happy and the Maestro was so contented. The orchestra's playing was incomparable. Now that I'm finished, I hope to start all over again!

Only now can I tell you that right from the very first day of my arrival I was able to understand what possibilities there are for me here. You can imagine how I lived in that time, I studied continually and my nerves stood up to it well. Right up till today I have been under continual pressure and tension. Altogether I have studied ... enough to remember for the whole of my life. Now it is finished, I am full of regret, I want to start again from the beginning.

Naturally, in the middle of this suffering, I have had satisfaction sufficient to bring me to seventh heaven. The things the Maestro has said and done will remain in my heart. If I were a writer I would be the only person able to write about the thoughts and torments which have passed through this great man. I'm quite sure he has told certain things to me alone.

Today I feel so light and sad! It's really finished. One can have in America so many failures but the satisfaction I had from these concerts can, I think, never be repeated. I need to say, that the surroundings here are new, and so different from ours. If I have firmly planted my nail here, next year we will have to hammer it in with all our force.

By the time of Guido's next letter, so much had occurred that his only means of telling Iris was by the use of numbered sections:

I'm no longer in my skin! I no longer have the strength, nor is my head in the right place to give you the news of today with calm and order, so please excuse me and read on:
1. London is offering six annual sessions for recording.
2. Victor had told me that, by the terms of its contract, the NBC Orchestra could record only with Toscanini [not strictly true: Stokowski and others recorded with the orchestra]. Toscanini has said: 'To hell with the contract' and that his orchestra is at my disposal.
3. A cable to London, to agree to conduct three sessions with the NBC, and three with an orchestra of my choice, when and where I want it.

Cantelli's recording contract had been arranged by David Bicknell, Manager of His Master's Voice, International Artists Department, via an American agent.

Section four of Guido's letter tells of an offer for him to become resident conductor of an orchestra "in a town in the south, whose name has escaped me." Section five, by far the longest, tells of further good fortune:

I was in the Maestro's studio when a telephone call came through from

Philadelphia — they have invited me for two concerts on the twenty-fifth and twenty-sixth of this month. The Maestro literally leaped from his seat, embraced me, kissed me and shouted, 'That is my real dream, I want them to get to know who you are.' Saying this he bounded about the studio full of enthusiasm and embraced me again. All those present were delighted and completely bowled over.

I'm thinking about Philadelphia — and that's not all — on the March 1st at Cleveland two other concerts, then others in a series. [The concerts at Cleveland did not materialise.] I'll explain — Munch is sick and all his concerts have been offered to me. The Maestro added, 'These days, I have been hoping someone would get ill, and you would be offered the opportunity of conducting without waiting for the next season — and it has happened.' So I've profited from someone else's bad luck.

Later Guido writes:

What is going on around me is truly incredible — telegrams with offers from all over the place — I don't know where to start! However, you can be at ease, the Maestro, Walter and Chotzinoff are very close to me. Walter has been with me at meetings for two whole days. From my handwriting you will notice my agitation but basically my brain is of one who comes from Piedmont — hard and sane. It is a time to decide many important things . . .

We read by chance some satirical comments in an article: 'Toscanini is so pleased by the performance of his *protégé* G. Cantelli that they celebrated yesterday by going to see the "Rockettes" without their wives.' In fact we are going tomorrow evening and we thought we were the only ones who knew. But America loves these little things as one soon discovers.

The "Rockettes" are the famous ballerinas, with legs of equal length. This orgy(!) was organised personally by the Maestro; can you imagine Toscanini and myself seeing this variety performance? He convinced me that I should not leave America without seeing this spectacle at the Radio City, probably because he wanted to go himself — in any case he's happy to be accompanying me.

No account exists of Guido's reactions to the "Rockettes," instead we are told of a new acquaintance:

At Philadelphia, Alexander Merowitch will be with me and will be my personal agent for the coming year. He is a dear person, and already the agent for Milstein, Horowitz and others. He is a Russian and everybody including the Maestro is happy with this solution, because it is difficult not to fall into the hands of organisations which exploit the people they are responsible for without any artistic sense.

Since Alexander Merowitch will be my agent, it will be me who is responsible for my actions. I will try not to make any false step in my career. You know that I am very stubborn. To work little and well in the best places is the secret — although for many this remains just an ambition.

Before going to Philadelphia, Guido found himself with some free
time:

The Maestro and I have watched many programmes on the television. We
have talked about Novara — he has fond memories of the town. He remembers
1889 and told me about it as if he was trying to get me embroiled in it! He
told me the names of many people from Novara (who by now must be dead)
from that period. He can remember so much, with the most incredible detail.

From tomorrow I will start to study for Philadelphia. In the meantime,
I will benefit from the rehearsals of Toscanini at the NBC. On a visit to
Carnegie Hall I met Stravinsky, conducting a concert of his music with the
Boston [Symphony] Orchestra — an absolutely stupendous orchestra.

Another experience. I have just returned from a great dinner given in
honour of de Luca, in a large club. I had to put on my evening dress and
there were 600 people there! The fittings in this club are absolutely fantastic,
but how boring the evening was. I was on the list of four or five guests of
honour. At a certain point in the meal the head of the house in his speech
named these guests and one by one we had to get up and acknowledge the
applause. I felt all their eyes on me after the presentation: few among those
present would have seen me conduct, but I think all of them knew of me
— however little. In that moment, I was one of the men of the day. Do
similar things happen in other countries as well? It was quite an experience,
despite my negative feelings and I will know how to behave at future
invitations.

. . . I escaped with the Maestro. After the meal we went on to the
terrace where there was sun and three beautiful tom-cats with the movements
of faithful dogs. At one point the Maestro, when encouraging me about
Philadelphia, sat down on the parapet of the terrace as only a kid of thirteen
years can do. How dear he is, and what simple words he told me in respect
of my leaving tomorrow. For him, I am the only conductor who has studied
the scores as seriously as he does. In sum, it was a warm day that I will not
easily forget. The more I tell the Maestro, the stronger is my desire to work
and to study with all my will which as you know by now has no limits.

And so to Philadelphia:

Today the first of two rehearsals at Philadelphia. I have got so many things
to tell you but, as usual in these cases, I don't know where to start. You'll be
asking me how the orchestra was? Naturally good, as everybody knows. But
after one rehearsal, above all a first rehearsal — there were two of them, but
the short interval made them seem as one — I have not really managed to
assert my full authority over them. I can't really say that everything went for
the best but don't let this upset you, you know what a pessimist I am. I only
want to say this: the NBC is not America. That orchestra has been playing
for more than ten years under Toscanini and it suffers from it — and rejoices
in it.

There follows a comment on the Philadelphia Orchestra's style of
playing:

The rhythms are very different and they are very strong on humour, which is something that, to a certain degree America brings to the fore — from its President right down to the last American. Naturally the first encounter between these people and I could not be really happy because although they are young, I feel myself — as a European — older than they. In a particular way I suffer, as they do not know how to suffer.

However, it is good that, before returning to Europe, I have had this meeting. Tomorrow with this experience over, I will think better and I feel certain that we can meet each other halfway — or, better still, win them completely over to my side, with me moving towards their view of things.

After the second day's rehearsal, both conductor and orchestra appeared to be moving in the same direction, as Guido writes:

Today it's better. I have to tell you in all sincerity . . . I am going through a terrific experience. Don't get alarmed — wait patiently for tomorrow's letter.

The Maestro told me on the telephone that I have got the strength of Hercules! Tomorrow I have to hope for a complete success because what I managed to do at rehearsal this morning I will always remember as a miracle. I won — I brought the orchestra over to my side.

What Cantelli achieved at rehearsal was repeated at the concert:

The concerts at Philadelphia have been something really extraordinary. The orchestra played so well it even surprised me — and that's saying something. The enthusiasm of the packed hall was very moving.

As soon as I got back to the hotel I telephoned Toscanini who, and this is something very touching, picked up the receiver himself straight away — he had been waiting for my call for half an hour and he was eager to hear everything. Tomorrow afternoon, when I get back to New York, I'll go straight to his place.

The next letter was written from Toscanini's house:

Here I am again at Riverdale, all radiant after my success at Philadelphia. Now there are only four days before I go. I have got a world of things to think about and do. Before next Wednesday, I'm going to record the Haydn [Symphony No. 93].

Cantelli's first recording session took place on March 2 in Studio 8H with Richard Mohr producing. In his final letter, Guido describes the session and his last hours in America:

The first few records have been made, but what heavy work. Listening to them again, the sound is good and even the performance is acceptable. There are two or three rather imprecise passages, which left a rather bitter taste in my mouth and for that reason I have not given the go ahead but the technicians hope to arrange things for me. It'll cause a delay in the issue of the record, but I want my first to be good.

After that I went with the Signorina Carla [Mrs. Toscanini], Margherita and the Maestro to supper. Finally they accompanied me to the hotel. I can't describe to you the goodbye scene. Toscanini was at the peak of emotion, throughout the evening he had been saying: 'Margherita, our son is leaving us, our son is leaving us.' With tears in my eyes and a knot in my throat, I kissed and embraced him, and the Maestro reciprocated with as much emotion.

In these last hours at the hotel, Toscanini continued to tell me everything he thinks about me, smiling and embracing me at each moment. Everybody is sad at my going, and I am as well — and how much! But the thought of returning to your arms makes me smile and I must think about our meeting now.

As if echoing Guido's sentiments, Toscanini felt the need to put his feelings towards Guido into words. As Guido departed, he wrote to Iris:

My Dear Iris:
Allow me to treat you with affectionate friendship and to tell you the joy that I am feeling when thinking about the return to Italy of my dear friend Guido and of our meeting. He's returning with the affection and admiration of all those who have been close to him and admired him — and there were many of them — not to mention the American public.

I personally have to tell you, that it is the first time during my long career as an artist that I have found a young person who is truly endowed with that indescribable but genuine quality which brings an artist to the top, very much to the top . . .

A warm embrace, yours devotedly
Arturo Toscanini

*

On his return voyage, Guido struck up a friendship with film producer Jack Cummings and his wife Betty, the daughter of composer Jerome Kern. Arriving in Italy, they were introduced to Iris and spent a delightful couple of days sightseeing with the Cantellis before attending concerts that Guido was giving in Bologna. When Jack Cummings saw how painfully cramped were the living conditions at Via Livorno he offered Guido a sum of money that would enable him to rent a larger apartment. After deliberating, Guido accepted. They did not move very far, as their new apartment overlooked the conservatory whereas at Via Livorno the church of Santa Maria alla Passione had been between them. Unfortunately for Guido, the new apartment building was inhabited almost exclusively by professors from the conservatory who all seemed to be working with their pupils at the same time. Guido found his concentration seriously disrupted and try as he might to seal himself off the very hot weather only made the situation worse. Shortly after the move further space became vacant at Via Livorno 5 and the Cantellis had no hesitation in returning to their old address.

In many ways, Jack Cummings epitomises the classic Hollywood rags-to-riches story. Joining Metro-Goldwyn-Mayer as an office boy he progressed to the script department, later becoming an assistant director, then a fully fledged producer. Jack Cummings's best-known work as producer is the musical *Seven Brides for Seven Brothers* (1954). He obviously thought that Cantelli's life was potential film material and both Guido and Iris were staggered when a telephone call came through from Hollywood with a proposal to make such a film. There is no evidence to suggest that Jack Cummings instigated the film on behalf of MGM, the offer may well have come from an independent producer, approached by Cummings. In due course a writer and secretary arrived at Via Livorno and began interviewing Guido. To his surprise, they were more interested in how he made love than in music! This was as far as the project went but for allowing it to go so far Guido received a considerable fee in dollars. History does not relate whether Guido would have played himself or not but the nearest Guido ever came to a film studio was in 1955 on tour with the New York Philharmonic when their concert in Los Angeles presented Jack Cummings with the perfect opportunity to escort his friends around the MGM lot at Culver City.

*

Toscanini was present at Teatro alla Scala when Cantelli directed a concert on June 1, made up of the works by Wagner, Franck and Bartók which he had performed with the NBC Symphony. On the twenty-sixth, Guido conducted the Scala Orchestra at Teatro Coccia. For Toscanini powerful emotions were aroused by this theatre as he explained to Guido in a letter written on the day of the concert:

> My Dear Guido:
> I am very sorry not to be with you this evening, but you know why — even at my age I still suffer timidity. However, I will be close to you with heart and soul and will join my applause to that of the people of your town who honour you in that theatre, in which I, not yet twenty-two years old, had the pleasure of my inauguration during the carnival of 1888/9. Oh what a marvellous time it was!
>
> Yours
> Arturo Toscanini

Whenever and wherever Cantelli was performing Toscanini would send a simple telegram before the concert reading "God bless you."

By the summer of 1952, Guido's finances were sufficient for him to rent for the season "Genzianella Alpino," a converted stable at Stresa, with a panoramic view over Lake Maggiore to the distant Alps. Here Guido planned and studied programmes for the coming season. He was, "very happy," recalled Mariangela Cantelli who visited "Genzianella" with her parents, taking time off from study and enjoying to the full the alpine situation. Mariangela has a particular reason for the extremely close affection she felt for Guido — and still does — as she explained: "I was born in the house where Guido was born. After I was born, I was put in his bed with him, so I started breathing his air from the beginning."

An extraordinary story concerning Cantelli and Toscanini, found its way into print after the summer of 1952, and Mariangela was able to confirm as an eyewitness its authenticity. Living at Stresa was no mere whim on Cantelli's part for he could gaze over Lake Maggiore and see Isolino di San Giovanni. One evening during a telephone conversation with Toscanini it was suggested that as they were so close it might be possible to see each other's house if they rapidly switched on and off a prominent light. When it was discovered that this worked it did not take long for them to devise their own private version of Morse code. Throughout that summer they would end their conversations by flashing "good night."

Cantelli's career obviously gained momentum from his association with Toscanini but, inevitably, over the years a mystique has grown surrounding their friendship and the musical influence Toscanini exerted. A beautiful definition of the precise nature of Cantelli's relationship with Toscanini, came from Franco Mannino:

> Every musician is influenced by the other great musicians who are alive at the same time, both composers and interpreters. Beethoven was influenced by Haydn, Haydn by Mozart ... It is important to be near a very great personality, but for the good of the brain not of the technique. For a violinist or pianist, a teacher is very important for the technique, but not for a conductor because the gesture is personal.
>
> For Guido to be near Toscanini was very important, because Toscanini always spoke music, and Toscanini's experience was great — over sixty years ... When you are near a genius, if you are intelligent, then you learn — you learn from his experience.

For Toscanini, Guido Cantelli was the biggest talent ever to cross his path and generally speaking he was in complete agreement with everything the younger musician did. However, there were aspects of Cantelli's work that brought forth vehement disagreement from the old man. He could not be reconciled to Guido's selection of the contemporary works that regularly featured in his programmes. To him, they represented — as we should say — Guido's attempt to be "with it" and not be looked upon as a conductor who stuck to well trodden paths, ignoring the music being written around him. Cantelli's method of study also irritated Toscanini for whom the six or seven hours Guido spent pouring over his scores each day amounted to little more than memorising, leading Guido to adopt a cerebral approach to music that left him wrapped in its pure mechanics. He was cutting himself off from reality and Toscanini

Angela Riccardone (courtesy of Mariangela Cantelli)

Antonio Cantelli (courtesy of Mariangela Cantelli)

Above *The Seventeenth Artillery Regimental Band, with their bandmaster Marshal Antonio Cantelli (seated with baton) (courtesy Mariangela Cantelli). Below Guido Cantelli's birthplace, the ground floor apartment at Via San Gaudenzio, 19. The tablet set into the wall was erected by the Novara authorities (photo: Laurence Lewis)*

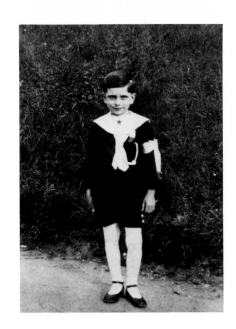

ove *Cantelli at two years (courtesy of*
ıriangela Cantelli). Above right
ntelli at six dressed for his
:firmation (courtesy of Mariangela
ntelli). Right *Felice Fasola — a*
otograph taken towards the end of his
* (courtesy of Andreina Fasola*
lizzari)

Above *Teatro Coccia seen from across Piazza Martiri della Liberta. Dominating the skyline is Antonelli's Cupola atop the Basilica di San Gaudenzio.* Below *Cantelli with his choir pictured in Rome around the years 1939 to '41. He can just be glimpsed in the centre of the back row, and appears to be the only member not wearing the fascist uniform (courtesy of Mariangela Cantelli)*

*Iris Bilucaglia at twenty
(courtesy of Mariangela
Cantelli.*

*Cantelli pictured shortly
after his marriage with
(right) brother Giuseppe
and behind (left to right) a
serviceman friend, Iris, and
his parents (courtesy of
Mariangela Cantelli)*

Above *Cantelli stands before the bill announcing his debut at Teatro alla Scala (From the collection of Leonard Myers, courtesy of Adele Cohen). Below January 1949: Cantelli with Toscanini (courtesy of Stuart and Jean Agrell)*

Above *Owen Mase (courtesy of Stuart and Jean Agrell)*. Below *1952: An evening with Toscanini at Riverdale. Seen with him are (back row, left to right) Frank Miller, Samuel Chotzinoff and Remo Bolognini. (Centre, left to right) Toscanini, Ben Grauer, Leonard Myers, Pauline Chotzinoff — sister of Jascha Heifetz — a member of the NBC Symphony and Alexander Merowitch — whose wife took the picture. (Front, left to right) Don Gillis, Iris Cantelli, Cantelli and Nicoletta Braibanti — niece of Pizzetti (from the collection of Leonard Myers, courtesy of Adele Cohen)*

Above left *"Follow my gesture"*: Cantelli in rehearsal with the Scala Orchestra *(1956)*. Above right *". . . he had very good balance, and used his arms and hands very expressively — huge hands, you know, with very long fingers"* (Manoug Parikian). Cantelli photographed during a concert at La Scala in June 1954 (photos: Erio Piccagliani, Teatro alla Scala)

was forever telling him to put away his scores and just look around. Walking through woods, gazing at fields, rivers, animals, buildings, pictures — even pretty girls — would bring him closer to the heart of a work of music than simply committing the notes "fly specks" he called them, to memory. When Toscanini spoke in this manner, Guido would go very quiet, like a schoolboy reprimanded by a favourite teacher.

Once, unintentionally, Guido deeply hurt Toscanini. After the NBC broadcasts, Guido and Iris would be driven to Riverdale for dinner. The evening's programme had included Brahms's First Symphony which Toscanini had listened to on the radio (he never attended the actual concerts), and greatly enjoyed. Coming forward to embrace and congratulate Guido in the hallway, his smile beaming approval, Toscanini was dumbfounded when Guido blurted out: "My Brahms one is the best around." Mortified, the Maestro sat in silence throughout the meal, which all present longed to finish. Cantelli's approach to music was faultless, but sometimes his approach to life outside the concert hall betrayed the lack of contact with reality which Toscanini so often warned him about. It was unfortunate that Toscanini should be a victim of that very defect.

Toscanini's sessions with Cantelli were very informal with there was never any thought of closeting Guido at the NBC or Riverdale and going through a particularly troublesome work, noting the difficulties and how they should be interpreted. He would take Guido aside in the living room, sit in his armchair and go through a piece. Usually these deliberations were so absorbing that repeated calls for meals would go unanswered.

Fasola, Ghedini, then Toscanini? "I think if Cantelli didn't know Toscanini, Cantelli still become Cantelli." (Franco Mannino)

*

Toscanini would be eighty-seven by the time he conducted the final concert of the 1953/1954 NBC Symphony season on April 4. Cantelli directed his last concert with the orchestra on February 21, culminating with a staggering account of the Beethoven Fifth that had the audience in Carnegie Hall wild with excitement. Few who heard it — audience or listeners over the air — could have doubted that Cantelli had proclaimed himself Toscanini's successor as principal conductor, and that this great orchestra was now his. He would conduct it once more on April 6, when they assembled in "Carnegie" to record Franck's D minor symphony. Toscanini must have discussed with Cantelli the possibility of announcing his retirement and that when he stepped down the orchestra would be disbanded. He was, after all, its *raison d'être*, without his presence there seemed little point to its programmes in NBC's radio schedules and gentle pressures were being applied with a view to hastening his decision.

Toscanini planned his 1953/1954 season to be a panorama of his life's work. Composers represented included Verdi, Beethoven, Richard Strauss, Tchaikovsky (the Sixth Symphony, relayed in experimental Stereo) and Boito. Spread over the season, the concerts lead up to a final Wagner programme on April 4. Just before the first rehearsal, Toscanini made a formal announcement of his resignation and faced his beloved orchestra knowing it to be the end. Although the works were familiar to the musicians, through numerous Toscanini performances over the years, there were fraught moments at the rehearsals, as he coped with the music and the enormity of his decision. When demand for tickets continued long after the hall was sold out, the final dress rehearsal was opened to the public who were told not to applaud. A matter of contention arose over where the orchestra should pick up a passage in the *Tannhauser* overture and, as if not caring, Toscanini walked off stage, leaving the work only partly rehearsed as he did not return and the rehearsal broke up.

When Toscanini conducted this work at the concert on the following day, everything went well until the bacchanale section. Here, the music seemed to go out of control: Toscanini just gave up conducting. Standing, as if in a trance he appeared to fight to recall his place in the score, at that moment erased from his memory. For about thirty seconds the performance fell to pieces. Cellist Frank Miller tried in desperation to conduct, then, dramatically, Toscanini pulled himself together, bringing the work to its conclusion. Hardly waiting for the applause, Toscanini then plunged straight into the *Meistersinger* prelude, walking off the platform at the end, never to return.

For those in Carnegie Hall the drama on stage appeared as one of those mishaps that can occur in the course of any concert but, via the radio, it must have sounded as if an unspeakable tragedy had taken place. As the performance fell to pieces, listeners heard the voice of Ben Grauer — regular presenter of the NBC Symphony broadcasts — explaining that technical difficulties necessitated an interruption of the relay. The broadcast faded, and listeners heard the opening bars of Brahms's First Symphony, conducted by Toscanini. Hardly had these sounded, when they too were faded, and the live relay continued.

Confusion surrounds these desperate minutes, with conflicting accounts from those who were present. Cantelli appears to have been back stage. Witnessing the drama on stage he ran upstairs to the NBC control booth, which overlooked the stage. Bursting in, he told Don Gillis, the producer, "Take him off, it's a disaster." Against his better judgement, Gillis had the broadcast faded and the record substituted — a turntable being kept ready for such an emergency. By this time Toscanini had already recovered and Cantelli had not in fact prevented the bad parts being relayed, he had only aggravated the situation. In the heat of the moment, could Guido have forgotten this was also a public concert and thought only of the radio audience? By imposing his will on the broadcasters, he made a terrible mistake. If indeed, it had been the tragedy he feared, Cantelli should have rushed on stage, where he could have rendered assistance to his ailing friend. But faced with such a predicament, who could blame him for the action he took.

*

In order to release on record Toscanini's broadcasts of *Aida* and *Un ballo in maschera,* a few re-takes were necessary. Accordingly, several months after the debacle of April 4, the NBC Symphony was specially reconvened. It was not a happy session and, although Toscanini went through the motions an air of gloom prevailed. Herva Nelli sang two arias from *Aida,* which became the last music Arturo Toscanini conducted: by a massive stroke of irony it had also been the first in 1886.

THE GARDEN OF MUSIC

As the strikingly modern Royal Festival Hall took shape, critics of London's new concert hall began to voice their fears. It was, they said, "utter madness," to build a concert hall on the south bank of the Thames at Waterloo where it would be isolated and attract sparse audiences. Its architecture by Robert Matthew did little to inspire confidence either. In order to establish the hall from its opening, and secure its future as Britain's premiere concert hall, the management wanted an event of major importance: they wanted Toscanini.

With the opening due to take place at the same time as the 1951 Festival of Britain, Owen Mase, the hall's Concerts Adviser, had been despatched to Milan with the brief to arrange a meeting with the Maestro. Toscanini's last concerts in London, with the BBC Symphony Orchestra, in Queens Hall, had taken place during the London Music Festival of 1939, organised by Owen Mase. As musical executive under Adrian Boult's direction at the BBC, Mase had led the negotiations that first brought Toscanini to the BBC Symphony in 1935, and thereafter in 1937, 1938 and 1939. As a result, Toscanini had come to look upon Owen Mase as his personal representative in Britain.

After attending two performances of the Verdi *Requiem*, given by La Scala forces under the direction of Toscanini, on June 26/27, 1950, Owen Mase wrote in his report to John Shove, the Royal Festival Hall's manager:

Although 83 years old he conducted these two consecutive performances of this enormous work and had a great party after each one, without any apparent diminution of energy — a very remarkable man — and I know no other conductor of any age who would not have shown considerable signs of wear and tear.

During his stay in Milan, which lasted from June 24 to July 1, Owen Mase saw Toscanini on several occasions. Together they worked out a programme of three concerts, as he details in his report:

He has finally decided that he wants to open the hall with the Beethoven Ninth Symphony. This great song of brotherhood he feels is absolutely right for the occasion and also provides that *mise-en-scène* necessary for a great occasion with its chorus, orchestra and soloists. He agreed to do the three programmes that we want and they are as follows:

First Concert — April 30th, 1951.

> Beethoven: Symphony No. 1
> Beethoven: Symphony No. 9

Second Concert — May 2nd, 1951.

> Kabalevsky: Overture *Colas Breugnon*
> Vaughan Williams: Symphony No. 6
> Strauss: *Don Juan*
> Debussy: *La mer*

Third Concert — May 4th, 1951.

> Beethoven: Fantasia for Piano, Orchestra and Chorus
> Beethoven: Symphony No. 9

Toscanini particularly wanted to include in his programme an important British work and, prior to their meeting, Toscanini had received from Owen Mase a score of what was then Vaughan Williams's latest Symphony, which the Maestro was very keen to perform. So London would be getting a Toscanini *première*, but at what price? In his report, Mase goes on to discuss this aspect of his deliberations with Maestro:

> On the last occasion he came to London for me he was paid £800 a concert. That of course, was in 1939, before the war. His fee in America at the moment is £1,200 a concert. I am glad to say that I was able to arrange with him to come and do these concerts for us at a total fee of £2,500. I naturally told him how much we appreciated his consideration of conditions in England.

Despite Owen Mase's careful planning, the concerts were not to be: the dying Carla asked to spend her last days in Milan and, for Toscanini, himself feeling unwell, her absence was unbearable. In February 1951 he cancelled all his outstanding engagements, leaving in mid NBC season to join Carla in Milan, where she died in June.

Members of all the London orchestras, together with sections of various choirs active in the capital, joined for the Royal Festival Hall's official opening concert, given on May 3, before an audience that inlcuded the King and Queen. Short works by Handel, Parry, Vaughan Williams, Elgar and Purcell were conducted by Sir Adrian Boult and Sir Malcolm Sargent. Sargent had recently succeeded Boult as principal conductor of the BBC Symphony Orchestra and he performed with one change of programme — the Brahms *Academic Festival* Overture in place of the Kabalevsky — the works which Toscanini would have given.

There was hardly an aspect of music that Owen Mase had not touched upon during his career. He was born in 1890, and music occupied his life from childhood. He studied at the Guildhall School of Music under Professor James Partridge, whilst simultaneously receiving piano lessons privately under Walther Knauss. As an accompanist, Owen Mase drew excellent reviews from newspapers and periodicals as important as "The Times," "Musical Times," "Daily Telegraph" and "Morning Post." In the years leading up to the First World War and in the early twenties, piano pieces, songs — which still receive the occasional performance — choral and orchestral music was published bearing his name. Then, in 1927, on the threshold of a distinguished career as composer and performer, he quit and, changing directions, forsook the life of an itinerant musician to join the BBC's music department.

With the formation of the BBC Symphony Orchestra in 1930 by Adrian Boult (he was knighted in 1937), Owen Mase became his musical executive, attending to the orchestra's repertoire, visiting conductors and soloists. Conductors in those early years included Sir Henry Wood, Bruno Walter, Felix Weingartner, Richard Strauss, Serge Koussevitsky and Toscanini.

During Toscanini's 1938 season, Oxford University wanted to confer an honorary degree upon him, as Owen Mase recalled in an article "Memories of the Maestro," published in the March 1957 edition of "Music and Musicians," (the Toscanini memorial number):

> ... the late Sir Hugh Allen asked me if I could possibly get him to give a concert at Oxford in aid of the funds for preservation of the fine old buildings of the University.
>
> The University wanted to mark the occasion and pay him honour by conferring upon him a high honorary degree. Several times during two or three days I broached the subject but could make no headway at all. I worked out a timetable that would allow of the visit being fitted in, and he agreed that it could be done, but he would simply not consent. Knowing his generosity in so many good causes I was puzzled at the refusal and tried to think of the reason.
>
> Then one evening his wife whispered to me that she thought it might be the conferring of the degree that was worrying him. I decided to ask him outright if this was the trouble. It was! It all came pouring out — about the procession, the wearing of gowns and all the pomp and ceremony which he knew would be involved. The crowning horror appeared to be "I would have to wear a funny hat!" If the degree were dropped, he said, he would be so happy "to come and conduct a concert for you anywhere for nothing."
>
> I rang up Sir Hugh and it was agreed to abandon the idea of the degree, much as the Univeristy would have liked to honour him. That trouble out of the way, the Maestro immediately consented. The BBC lent its orchestra and a wonderful concert resulted in a large sum for the funds.

What Owen Mase failed to add by way of a pendant to that article, was that with Toscanini's refusal of the degree, the University conferred it upon him instead.

After ten years Mase left his position at the BBC, becoming Director of Opera at Sadlers Wells Theatre. He kept performances on stage nightly, along with Sunday concerts, until the German bombing raids in 1940 made it impossible to continue, and the theatre was taken over as a public shelter.

Before the threatened aerial bombardment of London turned into reality, the BBC evacuated its orchestra to Bristol (this occurred in 1939, some months before raids commenced). With the orchestra away from London, the BBC felt unable to mount a Promenade Concert season during 1940. Since 1927, the BBC had assumed responsibility for each annual season at Queen's Hall, where they had run uninterrupted since their foundation in 1894. As late as December 1939, the BBC were still in two minds as to whether they should go ahead with the 1940 season but when, after much prevarication, Queen's Hall was approached for a booking, the BBC were told the hall had been let throughout the period they required. Reluctantly, they announced there would be no "Proms" that year. At which point, an extraordinary episode occurs in Owen Mase's life.

Joining forces with concert agent Keith Douglas, the Royal Phil- harmonic Society and Chappells, the lessors of Queen's Hall — who promised support — Mase set about organising a season for 1940. Early on, Sir Henry Wood had consulted with Mase and Douglas about keeping the concerts going and between them details were worked out in a matter of hours. Sir Henry then announced this would be his last season as chief conductor and that, after forty-six years, he thought that it was now time to hand over to a younger musician. He qualified his statement by adding that he had no intention of retiring completely. (Wood may also have issued this statement to gain extra publicity for the season.)

A popular season along conventional "Prom" lines was planned, running from August 10 until October 5, with the London Symphony Orchestra replacing the BBC Symphony. There were the usual nights devoted to a particular composer and an impressive number of first performances of works by British composers including Ralph Vaughan Williams, Lennox Berkeley, Edmund Rubbra, Elisabeth Lutyens, Frank Bridge, Cyril Scott, William Alwyn, Elizabeth Maconchy, together with other composers now forgotten. Soloists included Beatrice Harrison (Elgar's Cello Concerto), Myra Hess (Beethoven's *Emperor* Concerto), Benno Moiseiwitsch (Rakhmaninov's *Rhapsody on a theme of Paganini*), Eva Turner (Wagner) and, among others, Albert Sammons, Lionel Tertis, Clifford Curzon, Louis Kentner, Olive Zorian and Dr. George Thalben-Ball were prominently featured. Despite the limited amount of time available, Mase and his colleagues had assembled a season little different from those organised by the BBC.

Originally the concerts were timed to start at eight o'clock, but at the request of the authorities, from September 1 they were put back to six-thirty. Audiences flocked to Queen's Hall, breaking all previous box-office records but, alas, the radio audience was deprived of sharing in the experience as none of the concerts was broadcast. Many times during the season an air-raid warning sounded whilst a performance was in progress; when this occurred an unofficial impromptu concert began at the close of the programme and continued until the "all clear" sounded. Occasionally these impromptu programmes lasted well into the early hours, earning them the title of "Siren Sessions." Once as Sir Henry led the London Symphony Orchestra through a long Wagner evening a raid commenced and was still going on as the final bars were reached. Handing over the baton to Basil Cameron, he invited members of the LSO to play a series of party-piece solos. It was not long before they were joined by those in the audience who felt like "having a go." As the session continued song books were handed out and Basil Cameron directed his audience in a sequence of sea shanties, with Owen Mase at the piano. Whatever the Germans aimed on London, it seemed inconceivable that Queen's Hall would ever be hit. On the afternoon of May 10, 1941, Malcolm Sargent conducted a performance of Elgar's *The Dream of Gerontius*: that night, Queen's Hall was totally destroyed.

With the 1940 "Proms" concluded, Mase received an RAF commission, becoming a founder member of the RAF Regiment, specially created to guard airfields. He had seen active service in the First World War, being enlisted in 1914 in the University and Public Schools Brigade of the Royal Fusiliers. Commissioned in 1915 to the East Surrey Regiment, then transferring to the Rifle Brigade, he crossed to France the following year, staying there until 1920 in the army of occupation. In five years service with the RAF, Owen Mase saw action in England, France, Belgium, Holland and Germany, where he commanded the wing of the regiment with twenty-fifth sector RAF. Something about service life appealed to him, not the formal military discipline, more the existence around it. This gave him the opportunity to organise music appreciation classes accompanied by concerts featuring musicians who were stationed with him. Between calls to duty, it gave him much pleasure to enthuse about music to his young recruits. An award, the OBE (Military), recognised his services in this field.

As London's musical life picked up its threads after 1945, Owen Mase became involved with operatic seasons mounted at the Cambridge Theatre and the Stoll (long since demolished). The London Music, Art and Drama Society promoted these seasons, and he worked as managing director for four years. There was much talk during these years of a new concert hall to replace Queen's Hall. Eventually, it was hoped, the new hall would not just replace Queen's Hall, but supersede it altogether.

The Royal Festival Hall had been built by the London County Council, who originally intended to operate it solely for their own purposes, without letting the hall to outside managements. Joining as Concerts Adviser in 1950, Owen Mase had in effect taken on the role of programme planner and this brought him into contact with all the London orchestras and concert agents. His first duty was to organise the opening concerts, to be followed by concerts throughout the Festival of Britain.

There was mention of two parties in Mase's report, the second had taken place at Via Livorno 5:

> After this second performance there was another party which lasted until 3.30 a.m. This party was at Maestro Guido Cantelli's house and I was very interested to meet and make friends with this young conductor of thirty who is outstanding . . . You will remember Toscanini took him to America to conduct with him the NBC orchestra.

As their first meeting had taken place in a room full of people, conversation had been difficult so, before he left Milan, Owen Mase saw Cantelli again:

> I . . . had a further talk with Maestro Cantelli and he could be free in the Spring of 1952 to conduct a few concerts for us here, and he assured me that his fees would be made as low as possible because he is very interested in our new hall and could work it in on his way back to Italy from America. Cantelli, at thirty years of age, impressed me very much. We talked much music and he is a fine musician and very honest. I have not yet heard him conduct but we shall have the opportunity of hearing him in London in the Autumn of this year after he finishes at the Edinburgh Festival.

La Scala were bringing three productions, Verdi's *Otello* and *Falstaff*, conducted by Victor de Sabata, and Donizetti's *L'elisir d'amore*, conducted by Franco Capuana, for their first post-war appearances outside Italy, at the Royal Opera House, Covent Garden. A total of twelve operatic performances would be given, plus the Verdi *Requiem* (under de Sabata), which also formed the central point of their concerts in Edinburgh. Cantelli was given three of these; but with de Sabata and Capuana absent from La Scala on outside engagements, he took all the preliminary rehearsals. Cantelli's role on the tour was a very minor one, almost that of an apprentice trailing behind his master. In doing so, he was placing his talents before British audiences, something he had wanted to do since first approaching Major Arthur Watson back in April 1947.

Cantelli's first concert, on September 9, ended with a performance of the Tchaikovsky Fifth which electrified the audience in the Usher Hall, and became Edinburgh's festival sensation. Following his second concert, "The Scotsman" had written: " . . . Mr. Cantelli, has plainly the divine fire in him, but it is kept under fine artistic control." With people eager to discover this man with the "divine fire," tickets for his remaining concert were rapidly snapped up. In order not to disappoint those who were unlucky the festival arranged with La Scala for Cantelli to give a special Saturday morning concert, where he repeated his account of the Tchaikovsky Fifth, along with Monteverdi's *Magnificat*.

The Monteverdi, together with Mozart's *Requiem*, formed the concert that Cantelli was due to give at Covent Garden on September 22. On the night, a power cut resulted in the electronic organ being used in the Mozart going flat. As this was needed for the Monteverdi, Cantelli decided during the interval that he could not allow a performance with an instrument in this condition to take place, despite Covent Garden's attempts to rectify matters. On impulse he substituted Beethoven's Seventh Symphony, for the *Magnificat*. (The Scala Orchestra had performed this work under Cantelli at his second Edinburgh concert.) Because the works scheduled for performance only required a small orchestra, many of the players had taken the night off to see London or were seated in the audience. Frantic backstage efforts resulted in enough players being found for what amounted to an improvised performance. A dreadful lapse of ensemble following Guido's beat on the opening chords threatened to wreck all chances of a coherent performance. The players gripped their instruments and could be seen intently watching his every gesture, as he created an interpretation that relived Beethoven's inspiration bar-by-bar. It brought the house down, and he added Verdi's Overture to *I vespri siciliani* as an encore.

La Scala's operatic performances attracted only luke-warm reviews, but their orchestra excited the critics and they were coming more and more under the spell of their youngest Maestro. The shared experience of the Beethoven Seventh forged a bond between players and conductor: they felt they could trust him and that in turn, Guido felt able to ask and receive, knowing that they were his players to mould and shape as he desired. The way Guido had led them through Beethoven's Seventh became a legend among La Scala's musicians, a story that was, on their return to Italy, lovingly recounted over and over again — and which no one tired of hearing.

Cantelli gave another performance of the Tchaikovsky Fifth in his concert at the Royal Albert Hall, on September 25. By far the most perceptive report came from Sir Beverley Baxter, writing in the "Evening Standard". In fact, he was the paper's theatre critic and a long-standing Conservative Member of Parliament. His remarks were prefaced by the comment that, judged by his normal critical terms of reference, Guido Cantelli's performance on the podium was that of a great actor. As to his qualities as a musician, it is worth quoting Sir Beverley in full:

. . . in appearance he looked rather like Frank Sinatra, although tails give a man more height than a dinner jacket.

I shall never forget that performance of the 5th. It was one of the most exciting musical experiences of my life. Cantelli electrified the orchestra until they played like angels and devils.

We were not in Kensington but back in St. Petersburg of the Tsars. This young man had taken a worn-out symphony and had made it new with his own passion and genius. Quite rightly the audience went mad. A dozen times he came back to acknowledge the ovations . . .

De Sabata thinks Cantelli will be the greatest conductor in the World. So does Toscanini . . . so does the theatre critic of the "Evening Standard."

With an interpretation of the Tchaikovsky Fifth that poured out of him like molten metal from a crucible and that was received with acclaim by all who heard it, Guido was anxious to perpetuate his reading on disc. Whilst at Edinburgh he met David Bicknell personally for the first time and suggested the idea of a recording. However, it was not until they met again in London that a definite decision was taken to go ahead and record. This proposed recording presented something of a dilemma as La Scala's schedules had not taken into account the possibilities of any recording sessions taking place and, with a very restricted amount of time available, only two sessions were allocated, and these were held at Abbey Road Studios on the day of La Scala's final appearance at Covent Garden and on the day following Cantelli's Albert Hall concert. To arrange this, the orchestra remained behind in London for one extra day, while the rest of the company returned to Milan. For Cantelli then, it was make or break for, if he failed to complete the recording it would have to be aborted, as it was technically impossible to complete in Milan.

Tchaikovsky composed his Fifth Symphony for an orchestra of about eighty-five players: Cantelli was using around one hundred — virtually every musician La Scala had brought with them. Many of the wind parts in his version had been doubled or even quadrupled. Having used all these additional musicians on stage, Guido was naturally most keen for them all to take part in the recording: this, however, raised a problem. Large as the studio at Abbey Road was, it could not accommodate that number of musicians and still produce a satisfactory recording balance. David Bicknell diplomatically suggested to Guido that he would have to lose a few players before recording commenced but received the answer he had expected when Guido refused to contemplate the loss of even one player! Dr. Ghiringhelli tried to persuade Guido, knowing he was wasting his time and that nothing would make Cantelli change his mind once he knew what he wanted: one hundred players. Sensing the futility of carrying the argument any further, Cantelli's one hundred musicians assembled in the studio.

As with their concert performances, Cantelli and the orchestra performed Tchaikovsky's music as a seemingly unending stream of melody. Pleading, imploring, Cantelli drew forth the sounds, creating in the studio an atmosphere that reached fever pitch, with the violinists almost on their feet, as if encouraged by their Maestro to become soloists. As the clock ticked inexorably forward, the famous barnstorming coda brought the recording to completion in the closing moments of the final session, leaving a stunned silence in the studio.

Originally issued on 78's, the recording was subsequently transferred to LP, being among the first HMV Long Playing Records. When reproduced on modern equipment the recording quality has a boxed-in sound and lack of dynamic range, due to the vast number of musicians employed. Its recent reissue by World Records has, with more sophisticated cutting techniques, been able to open the frequency range and impart a bloom to the strings.

What spare time Guido had whilst in London (apart from the 1949 NBC season, Iris accompanied Guido to all his engagements) was spent in company with Owen Mase. Over a six year period, their friendship renewed itself each time Guido came to London for his seasons with the Philharmonia. It has been suggested that Mase's association with Toscanini allowed the Maestro to hint that Mase should look after Guido like a son each time he came to London. Certainly he took these duties seriously, being particularly on the watch for journalists out for a piece of racy copy on the young conductor. Wherever Cantelli went, so too did Owen Mase. Because of this, most people found it hard to get really close to Cantelli as a person, with Mase hovering in the background. Sometimes he gave the impression of holding Cantelli back, when his personality appeared to be asserting itself. There was nothing selfish in this attitude, Owen was a very well meaning person, who took his duties to Guido seriously, although it seems unlikely that he did actually receive instructions from Toscanini. Their friendship was a true meeting of minds.

All this was not to the exclusion of Iris, for she found a kindred spirit in Owen's wife Georgina. Although not an artist like Iris, Georgina Mase had a sensitive personality that responded to her surroundings. She felt passionately about nature, and loved trees, especially the beech. All her married life with Owen seemed to be spent moving from one place to another and she was thus able to observe nature from many new vantage points. Unlike Iris, who would have put her feelings for nature onto canvas, Georgina Mase expressed herself on film, in albums of beautifully composed shots of sunlight streaming to earth through branches. More intimate was her verse, through which her love of trees was put into words, at their finest in her published selection "Beeches Felled" and her anthology "The Book of the Tree." Iris and Georgina spent their time touring the London galleries, while Guido stayed behind at their hotel (the Cantellis always stayed at the Savoy when in London) studying between rehearsals. Although he knew that his scores were fully prepared, he was never "sure" enough and only once did he join them, on a visit to the Tate Gallery. No London season was complete without a weekend spent with Owen and Georgina at their cottage "Caniper Dell" in the heart of the Buckinghamshire countryside. Its very isolation afforded Guido precious moments of tranquility, as he gave himself to music.

By 1953 — Coronation year — a pattern of regular concertgoing at the Royal Festival Hall had become established and concert managements were begging the LCC to be allowed to stage their own events in the hall. It was decided to let the hall on a permanent basis. This allowed the London orchestras to plan their own seasons with dates alloted by the hall which retained overall responsibility for the day-to-day running. Effectively this terminated Owen Mase's position as Concerts Adviser. In his three years at the hall over 150 concerts had been planned and carried out by his office. He resigned, aiming to spend his time in semi-retirement, looking after Guido's affairs, performing a function similar to that he had provided for Toscanini.

Mase could not have foreseen a future in which the Maestro outlived his *protégé* and he never really got over the shock of Guido's death. For a time he kept up his musical contacts, useful in persuading friends to perform at a music circle he partly organised, but this interest did not last long and as it faded he lost interest in anything musical. He could understand Toscanini not being "there," even he was not immortal: Cantelli — no. So a man who had been at the centre of so much music slipped quietly into obscurity, forgotten except by a few close friends, who grew fewer and fewer as time passed. Only Alfred Kalmus, the music publisher, remained and they met at least once a year. When Georgina died in 1968 a further hole was bored into his emptiness. Occasionally he would rally, stimulated by a broadcast concert, perhaps by the playing of violinist Arthur Grumiaux whom he much admired. His collection of Toscanini and Cantelli recordings, however, stayed in their sleeves, mostly unplayed, shadows of the people he had known in life.

Owen Mase died in 1973.

*

Between September 1951 and July 1956, Guido Cantelli made twenty-five appearances with the Philharmonia Orchestra before packed audiences at the Royal Festival Hall. The 1953 season, however, took place in the Royal Albert Hall. S.A. Gorlinsky, sensing Cantelli's growing rapport with London audiences, and eager to take advantage of the thousands of visitors pouring into London for the Coronation on June 2, mounted his season there in mid-May. Cantelli also conducted three of the six concerts given by the Philharmonia at the 1954 Edinburgh Festival, the others being under Herbert von Karajan. These were all Cantelli's public appearances with the orchestra, but with three or four rehearsals for each concert together with his recording sessions over a five-year association, Cantelli logged a considerable number of hours making music with the orchestra.

When a conductor dies, we automatically feel his loss, yet somehow the essence of his life can be recreated through the legacy of his recordings. These can become almost like video-tapes of concerts, if the listener knows the conductor's interpretations from live performances. Orchestras on the other hand, go on forever. If a musician leaves or dies, he is replaced, his seat does not remain empty, but in the listener's mind it remains, over the years, the same orchestra. The Philharmonia of 1951 is not the Philharmonia Orchestra of 1978, as there has been, with the exception of one or two players, a complete change of personnel from the orchestra that played for Cantelli. Many of the musicians who played with Cantelli are still active as soloists, orchestral players and teachers.* A great number operate as freelance session musicians, taking part in anything from pop music to film scores; one or two are now too ill to continue playing; and in any discussion of the Philharmonia, the names of clarinettists Frederick Thurston and Bernard Walton, timpanist James Bradshaw and principal horn Dennis Brain, must be recorded.

In many ways the rise of the Philharmonia Orchestra from its foundation in 1945 parallels the meteoric career of the pre-War BBC Symphony Orchestra. Although only seven years old when Cantelli faced it for the first time, the orchestra had already acquired an awesome reputation, largely through its recordings which had taken the name "Philharmonia" around the world. In those days a public appearance by the orchestra was a musical event of the highest order, but even they were experiencing a certain amount of nervous tension waiting for Cantelli's first rehearsal. Everyone was very conscious of the aura surrounding Cantelli, built up by advance publicity, which laid great stress on his reputation as Toscanini's successor. At this period, the orchestra followed continental practice and had two leaders or concert-masters — Manoug Parikian (1949/57) and Max Salpeter (1949/56). Before each season, it would be decided who would lead for each individual conductor, although both appeared on stage. Manoug Parikian always led for Cantelli. He assessed the effect of this publicity:

> It certainly created perhaps the wrong atmosphere. That sort of publicity doesn't do good to anyone, and I felt Cantelli suffered for it a little. That he was hailed as the successor of Toscanini, or the future Toscanini — you know that does no one any good. In fact, wise and experienced conductors had been running away from that mantle — quite rightly too — because the mantle of Toscanini for instance when he resigned from the New York Philharmonic [Symphony] and the NBC, publicity anxious managers were only too eager to cast that mantle on to the nearest likely candidate. I had always had a feeling that perhaps Cantelli was a little bit unwise to accept

---

* When a musician is mentioned in the text the dates in brackets refer to his period of service with the orchestra.

that mantle, or make use of it, because if anything, it was to his detriment.

On the other hand of course, one must realise that he obviously revered Toscanini to such an extent, and admired him both as man and musician and conductor. I believe from all accounts Toscanini also admired Cantelli very much, and guided him through various scores, explaining to him what his feelings were to the music: so obviously that admiration was mutual. Well, all good things have bad side effects, and this is something Cantelli realised, and was prepared to put up with.

Despite his close proximity to Cantelli, Manoug Parikian never felt that he got to know him personally, even though they met on a few private occasions at his hotel for lunch or supper.

Mendelssohn's *Italian* Symphony opened Cantelli's debut concert at the Festival Hall on September 30. There were five concerts in the season, and in the final programme he included a complete performance of *Le quattro stagioni* by Vivaldi. In 1951, this piece — which today must be top of the "Baroque Ten" — can have been familiar to very few members of the audience, since performances were rare. Indeed it is safe to say that most of the people who attended the concert were attracted by the remainder of the programme, which contained works by Strauss, Sibelius and Rossini. That most were hearing the Vivaldi for the first time became obvious by the applause following each of the four concertos.

Whether one regards *Le quattro stagioni* as a single work, or a sequence of four violin concertos, they remain the only pieces with an instrumental soloist Cantelli ever directed with the Philharmonia. "I can't pretend I was a soloist in the true sense," recalled Manoug Parikian, who took the part, for unlike a true soloist, he sat with a music-stand in front of him between Cantelli and the orchestra's leader. "He asked me if I would like to do the Vivaldi *Seasons*, he thought it would go very well. I was thrilled of course to do it, but I can't remember much about the performances — that's the sad thing — it seems such a long time ago . . .

"A Young Great Conductor," ran Sidney Harrison's headline above his review in the now-defunct publication, "John O' London's Weekly." Harrison's lengthy article commented in turn on each work in the programme, saying this of the Vivaldi: "All through, Manoug Parikian played the solo violin part with unfailing elegance . . . The orchestra was magnificent . . . Somebody's magic must have been at work. I am not proclaiming any new discovery when I say that Guido Cantelli's conducting is rather more than good."

This concert was given twice, with Guido finding time in between to broadcast impressions of his first London season on the BBC Italian Service. They were heard during the "literary magazine" section of "La Voce di Londra" transmitted on October 12. Accompanied to the studios in Bush House by Owen Mase, Guido took part in an unscripted interview with Gwyn Morris. This appears to be his only serious radio interview, but tragically there is no transcript in the BBC's archives.

One radio interview does exist between Cantelli and Ben Grauer, who spoke to him after a Toscanini broadcast in February 1953. Despite Grauer's tendency to answer his own questions, Guido talks about his two forthcoming NBC concerts, and in particular — to Grauer's feigned surprise — the concert on February 28 which duplicated the very first he had given with the NBC Symphony, five years previously, and which he was repeating to mark the occasion.

At thirty-one, Cantelli was slim and of middle height with lovely wavy chestnut hair. Outwardly he did not look a strong person, delicate would be an apt description, but delicate in a way that a greyhound is delicate, capable of extraordinary feats of stamina, even taking a deep breath seemed to be an effort for him.

Cantelli's musical impact on the Philharmonia had the "impression of a time bomb," thought Clement (Clem) Relf, who since the orchestra's foundation has occupied the position of orchestral librarian. As Cantelli had to consult with him over particular editions of the works he was conducting and the markings he required, Clem Relf probably spent more time alone with Cantelli, than any other member of the orchestra. Although he could not recall his actual first meeting with him, the force of his personality was still extremely vivid: "A fantastic talent, I think so much talent, that physically he couldn't control it. After half an hour on the box, you'd think he was on the point of collapse. When he began to get worked up emotionally, it manifested itself physically, and sometimes he just had to stop and go off."

Cantelli's limited English caused him distress, as he felt it made communication difficult. In these opening concerts, as he was establishing an empathy with his musicians it is not surprising that his emotions sometimes got the upper hand. With apprehension pulling in one direction, music pouring out through every nerve, and Guido's subconscious relaying messages, that what he wanted to express about the music was not getting across to the orchestra. Fearing they would not understand him Guido attempted to explain in an almost child-like manner. "Look, I'm suffering because of what I've gone through," he gold them in his best English, "I know what I am, I'm not easy, do forgive me." They did. "They certainly felt for him, and sympathised for him, I'm sure of that, because there was so much respect for his talent. It was a great orchestra in those days, so there was a lot of respect on both sides. They made lots of allowances. If he got himself worked up, nobody got upset by it, but patiently carried on and that did help him a lot I'm sure." (Clem Relf)

Inevitably, with an orchestra of around ninety musicions, there are bound to be individuals who will disagree with their conductor and take a negative attitude towards his personality. They may be having problems with their instrument, which in turn leads to frustration when they are asked by the conductor to play a phrase in a certain fashion, which asks more of them than they are prepared to put into it at that moment. Technical problems had not beset Gareth Morris (1948/72), the orchestra's principal flute but he was not prepared to make musical concessions for Cantelli and virtually from their first rehearsal began a long-running feud. As Gareth Morris remembered, it started with an important solo near the beginning of Strauss's *Tod und Verklärung*: "I was just putting the flute to my lips when he almost screamed: 'It must be *piano* — *pianissimo*,' and I hadn't played a note. So, being a man of just as much temperament as he I immediately said: 'Look, I have not played anything, how can you tell me to play it quieter, when I haven't played a note.' Whereupon he, of course, blew up, and left the podium very upset." And he was to do likewise at one of his first recording sessions with the Philharmonia.

A group of sessions built around works given in the concerts, began at Abbey Road on October 13, with Tchaikovsky's *Romeo and Juliet*. Cantelli had given a brilliant performance of *La valse* at the Festival Hall and this was slated to follow, but it proved a catastrophic session.

A huge orchestra is necessary to do justice to Ravel's lavish orchestration. As Cantelli walked to the podium, musicians in the very full studio were putting the final preparatory touches of bows on strings and breath on reeds. Cellos and basses open Ravel's evocation with a rumbling deep in the instruments' compass, suggestive of an impenetrable haze. Something in what he heard displeased Cantelli about this passage, possibly intonation or phrasing, something was not the way he wanted it. For three-quarters of an hour, he reheased the cellos and basses in this passage until they reached the performance he desired. After paying attention to one or two more details in the score Cantelli felt that he had rehearsed sufficiently to attempt a recording. Before commencing, a word of caution was offered to Guido from the engineers. He was tending to emphasise the music's rhythmic pulse by tapping his feet on the podium and these sounds were being picked up by the microphones.

The recording buzzer sounded and the red light came on. Cantelli, baton poised, was ready to give a down beat, when the studio's double doors burst open to admit a double-bass player. This particular musician was not a regular member of the orchestra, only joining when extra players were required. By mistake he had gone to Kingsway Hall (where the orchestra did much of their recording, and virtually their home in these years) and, finding it empty, realised his mistake and made his way to Abbey Road, arriving somewhat late. "I'm very sorry, Maestro; I went to the wrong studio, please forgive me," he begged Cantelli, anxious to make amends. Cantelli said nothing. Taking this as a sign of forgiveness, the bassist flung his hat and coat in a corner, and began hastily setting up his instrument.

Once again the buzzer sounded and the red light came on. Cellos and basses waited, bows poised, for Cantelli's downbeat, for what seemed an eternity. Eventually it came, followed almost at once by a cry of anguish from Cantelli, calling upon all the saints to come to his assistance! Then, to everyone's amazement, he ran out of the studio — still calling on his saints. This outburst was triggered off not by the late arrival of the bassist, but by the musician's failure, in his haste to appease Cantelli, to tune his instrument, thereby ruining the passage so painstakingly rehearsed.

Inconsolable, Cantelli refused to be pacified by any of the recording staff. Only Iris could get anywhere near him, and it took much skill on her part, to restore him to the happy mood he had been in at the start of the session. No one dared to mention attempting another take on *La valse*, fearing that simply mentioning the work to Guido would provoke a relapse. Meanwhile the orchestra enjoyed a coffee break that stretched into a lunch break. By the time lunch was over, Guido had recovered sufficiently to think about recording again. *La valse* was out, he'd had enough of that work for one day; instead, he proposed they record the *Siegfried Idyll*. Perhaps Guido was being somewhat ironical in putting forward this piece, as Wagner's beautiful little masterwork requires only an orchestra of chamber proportions, whereas the Ravel demanded cohorts of players. After the fiasco of *La valse*, this session was pure magic. The Ravel remained unrecorded, although Cantelli continued to perform it throughout his career: but never again with the Philharmonia.

In the space of a few weeks, the Philharmonia had experienced the full force of Cantelli's personality. Their feelings towards him, were succinctly put by violinist Jean Lefevre (1947-60): " . . . personally, I was just frightfully interested, and immediately felt in sympathy with him . . . I felt that he wasn't always getting what he wanted, perhaps, and made one feel a little nervous and on edge you know, in trying to do what he wanted."

From that first season, Guido Cantelli became known to members of the Philharmonia as "The Little Boy." When he returned for his second season, exactly a year later, he would be preceded by Toscanini.

*

By 1952, Arturo Toscanini had more or less retired from the concert scene. Apart from his concerts with the NBC Symphony he undertook no more guest appearances. He did, however, conduct a Wagner programme at Teatro alla Scala, on September 19. As with all his post-war appearances there, Toscanini refused to take any fee. The concert marked the last occasion he would conduct at La Scala, although he did, as we shall see, plan to conduct one last opera there, as late as 1955.

The name "Toscanini" still carried with it an aura that no other conductor in history has ever had. After so long an absence from London, the slightest whisper that he might be returning was enough to launch a deluge of ticket enquiries. Because of the disappointment surrounding the cancellation of his concerts to open the Festival Hall, it was thought prudent that a suitable length of time elapsed before overtures were again made to entice the Maestro to London. It would be fascinating to read what correspondence passed between Toscanini and Owen Mase's office during this period. One can be sure that his close ties with Toscanini would have enabled Mase to keep in active communication regarding a new series of dates. Unfortunately, nothing survives relating to his office at the Festival Hall, either in the hall's own archive or in Owen Mase's private papers: only the report previously quoted, which was found amongst these. (The Festival Hall did have a file on Cantelli, but some years ago it appears to have become lost.)

Elated from his first concerts with the Philharmonia, Cantelli, as soon as he could, described the orchestra to Toscanini in glowing terms. Here was an orchestra fully worthy of the Maestro's talents which he must conduct at the earliest possible opportunity. Cantelli knew that time was running out for Toscanini, and he so fired the old man's imagination that he felt one last attempt should be made to arrange some concerts. Before coming to a final decision, however, Toscanini wanted to hear the orchestra in person, although he was not unaware of their reputation through their recordings. That chance presented itself in May 1952.

During May, Herbert von Karajan took the Philharmonia on their first European tour. On May 19/20 the orchestra gave two concerts at Teatro alla Scala. Toscanini, on holiday, attended one of these pro-·grammes with Cantelli. After the concert, La Scala's management gave a lavish reception for the orchestra, at which Cantelli was present looking very much at home in the Scala's plush atmosphere. Talking to members of the orchestra, he explained that Toscanini had heard the concert and sent apologies for not attending the reception as he was too tired. However, he had been impressed by their performance, and subject to the usual contractural formalities, he would come to London and conduct them. Negotiations proceeded rapidly and impresario S.A. Gorlinsky announced that Toscanini would direct a two-concert Brahms cycle at the Festival Hall on September 29 and October 1. Not unnaturally, demand for tickets far exceeded seating capacity, so a postal ballot — rather like that currently held for the first and last nights of the proms — was thought to be the fairest way of allocating the 6,000 seats, for which there were 50,000 applicants.

Six rehearsals were scheduled, divided between Kingsway Hall and the Festival Hall. At the first the entire orchestra was seated and tuned some considerable time before Toscanini's entrance: an occurrence that seems to be unique in British orchestral history! As they were new to him, the orchestra feared that an outburst of the famous Toscanini temperament could be expected if anything went wrong, but quite the reverse happened. There were no tantrums, no watches smashed to pieces (as had happened in front of the NBC Symphony); instead he was, in the words of one musician, "as nice as pie!" Only for one moment did a stamp of his foot and a blaze in his eye become apparent and this had the effect of putting the fear of God into the players. Mostly Toscanini spoke few words, repeatedly; "Cantare," ("It must sing.") He dispensed with one rehearsal completely, and was content with just a run-through of the Second Symphony. In contrast, he spent an inordinate amount of time on the Third Symphony, which he approached with a special affection. Following a rehearsal at the Festival Hall, Toscanini complained to Cantelli and Manoug Parikian that he could not hear sufficient string tone. They explained that a full complement of strings were present, and that perhaps the hall's dry acoustic, which he had not adjusted to, might be leading him to this conclusion. (Surprising, from one who adored the dry acoustic of NBC's Studio 8H.) In order to satisfy the Maestro, a few extra players were brought in, including Hugh Maguire and Neville Marriner.

Cantelli was present, at all times, appearing very much a pupil of the master. He followed minutely every detail of Toscanini's interpretations from the score, and learned a useful lesson when the Maestro brought a rehearsal to a premature end. Cantelli motioned that he should continue until the end of the allotted time, but Toscanini knew that any more time spent on the work would be over-rehearsal and so cut matters short. Cantelli saw to the orchestral seating and to the personal comforts the Maestro required. "It was like a father and son relationship, the whole way through it seemed to me. He adored Toscanini — no doubt about that — and the old man, I think, saw Cantelli as the continuation of himself, knowing that he was near the end of his time and Cantelli was at the right age to carry it on." (Clem Relf)

An incident at the first concert was to bring this forcibly home.

As originally planned, only the Brahms symphonies were to be performed, the First and Second in the first concert, the other two in the second, plus the *Variations on a theme by Haydn*. At the last moment the *Tragic Overture* was included in the first programme, very nearly causing a disaster. The overture was preceded by the National Anthem. Toscanini had not performed this since his last visit in 1939 and was only informed of its inclusion on his arrival at the hall. Manoug Parikian hastily took him through the piece but in all the confusion it slipped from Toscanini's mind that the concert would open with the *Tragic Overture*, directly followed by the First Symphony. Toscanini waited as the audience settled down after the anthem, then he gave two very slow down beats, while the orchestra expected to receive six quaver beats. For a couple of bars there was chaos as Toscanini conducted the First Symphony, and the orchestra played the *Tragic Overture*. Almost immediately Toscanini pulled to, the shock instantly restoring his memory. Cantelli, from his position in the stalls realised exactly what had occurred and during the interval tried to reassure Toscanini that it did not matter. A slip like that could happen to anyone: for Toscanini it was another sign that his previously infallible memory could let him down, and that time was slipping away.

No sooner were Toscanini's concerts over, than Cantelli began rehearsing for his second season with the Philharmonia. Toscanini, who stayed on in London for a couple of days, attended one of these. During a break, he chatted with the musicians as if he had been with them all his life. A rapport existed which he dearly wanted to prolong — if only he were ten years younger. These concerts were his last in London, and he left knowing that Guido's talents would find their highest expression through the musicians of the Philharmonia.

*

Now the Philharmonia had performed Brahms under both Cantelli and Toscanini, for the Third Symphony had been included in Cantelli's first season. Working with Toscanini remains a profound experience for Manoug Parikian, the Third Symphony particularly so: "I would be doing both of them an injustice, if I pretended that Cantelli's reading was as mature and as strong as Toscanini's — that simply wasn't so. What I remember of Toscanini's concerts with us, are his trememdously powerful, — even at that age — vital personality, but also his simple approach to music. Cantelli's approach to music was much more youthful, he was a young man, he had youthful exuberance and zest which an old man cannot have. Purely from the musical point of view, I cannot believe that Cantelli approached the basic strength of Toscanini's performances."

"Toscanini was much tougher," recalled violinist Marie Wilson (1948/63). She was among several members of the Philharmonia who had previously been with the BBC Symphony Orchestra and had played under Toscanini before the war. Marie Wilson's career goes back to the Twenties and Sir Henry Wood's Queen's Hall Orchestra — she led for him during the 1935 Proms — and she is still active in the London Philharmonic of today. For her, the Toscanini she had known was not an old man, but one in the prime of life, which perhaps explains her remark about him being "tougher." "He was a great genius, but he was a very much older and more experienced man. He could carry things, his temperament overflowed — he was more dynamic. This boy [Cantelli] had more emotion than learning."

"Emotion" from Cantelli, "strength" from Toscanini. In their quest for the truth behind the notes, both conductors spared no effort in trying to realise the intentions of the composers. This meant hard work for the players in producing the sound their conductors had in mind. This task was made easier by their beat, where they pointed the baton, there was the beat, unlike that of Furtwängler (who worked a lot with the

Philharmonia in his last years) which gave an impression of not relating to where the sound came from, causing a sensation of delayed or out-of-sync sound, Toscanini and Cantelli's beats were right on the pulse of the music. Nothing came between them and the music, it was a direct communication that could be felt instantly by any musician responsive to the emotions and strengths passing through them.

Literally nothing came between Toscanini or Cantelli and the music, for both conducted without a score. When Toscanini did consult the score his extreme myopia necessitated his peering at the notes inches from his nose. An affectation on Cantelli's part, which used to annoy some members of the Philharmonia, was his habit, when consulting the score at rehearsals, of imitating Toscanini by holding it inches from his nose. They all knew that every detail of the score was stored in his memory, and that he knew the answer without really having to look: Guido realised they knew this, but used the time to calm himself on occasions which might otherwise have precipitated an outburst of temper.

Cantelli's ability to be able to probe deep into the heart of a work and present it without putting himself before the notes in any form was commented on by Canadian violinist Arthur Davison (1950/57). Even at that stage of his career, Arthur Davison knew he wanted to become a conductor, and he is today closely associated with the Royal Philharmonic Orchestra and his own Virtuosi of England. His thoughts come not only from one who observed Cantelli on the podium, but also from his own experience. "My impression of him, was of a man very delicately balanced, who had studied the work, and understood the work to such a degree, that it was almost a laser beam. I think, if you put the word 'Laser Beam,' *vis-à-vis* his technique and his talent — in fact you could almost say his genius for making music — then you'd have him in a nut.

*

Four concerts were given in Cantelli's 1953 Philharmonia season: a season which proved to be a strictly Nineteenth-century affair, with nothing closer our own time than Dvořák's *New World* Symphony and the Tchaikovsky Fifth. Taking into account how near to the coronation these concerts took place, it does seem a pity that Cantelli did not — or was not asked to — include a work by a British composer in his programmes. Several eminently suitable works by Walton, Vaughan Williams and Elgar come readily to mind. (Guido's library, which Iris Cantelli still has, contains the following scores by Elgar: the *Enigma* Variations, *Falstaff*, the Violin Concerto and *Pomp and Circumstance* No. 1 — none of which he conducted.) Indeed, that criticism might apply in general to all the Philharmonia concerts. Works by American composers came under Cantelli's baton in the NBC and New York Philharmonic Symphony concerts and he did have one major British work in his repertoire, the *Sinfonia da Requiem* of Benjamin Britten, which had already been given with the NBC Symphony and, more significantly, at La Scala. He was, however, probably told not to give this work in London, in case its appearance had dire consequences at the box office and, in fact there can have been few British conductors performing this work at the time.

This raises the whole question of Cantelli's repertoire; Iris Cantelli strongly refutes the oft-voiced criticism that it was too small: "I think for a man of thirty-six years when he died to have 250 scores by memory was not so small a repertoire." Compared with Toscanini's, Cantelli's repertoire inevitably appears small. New works came in gradually, there was never a rush to prepare a great many new scores at the beginning of each season. "That was his style of approaching music. There are musicians who will not think twice before embarking on a season with perhaps 150 works, Cantelli wasn't like that . . . I don't think this need be taken as a weakness in a conductor, after all, we only knew Cantelli over a period of four or five years [*sic*], and that's a very short time." (Manoug Parikian)

Almost as if to encourage the view that his repertoire was small, Cantelli was in the habit of repeating works again and again. There was a sound musical reason for this, as Iris Cantelli explained: "He loved the pieces so much, and to conduct a piece with one orchestra different from another, the piece changed completely, it became another thing. His idea was to play the same pieces with different orchestras in the same manner, but it was impossible."

Nevertheless, the feeling remains that he did perform certain works once too often although never in run-of-the-mill performances. This perhaps was Guido Cantelli's one failing: that he loved these works so much and could not bear to be parted from them. He felt there would be time for him to accomplish all he sought and to perform a work in public without knowing it down to its last nuance was not his way. Any conductor can acquire a vast repertoire, but that does not mean they understand with equal surety each and every work — Cantelli did!

*

Before embarking on rehearsals with the Philharmonia Guido would consult with Clem Relf about the orchestral material the orchestra had available. "He was one of these people you could go in and discuss: What are you going to do? What editions are you going to use? What markings? What bowings? All this kind of thing, which he'd prepare beforehand to try to make it as easy for him and them [the Philharmonia] as possible. All these ideas were down on paper — as far as one can put them on paper — then the rest had to happen at rehearsals. I think he took that side of it very seriously, and he was marvellous to work with, I must say."

Cantelli's desire to know every detail of a work encompassed not only the full score, but all the orchestral parts, to which he brought just as much care and attention. For Cantelli, being conductor meant having the interpretative knowledge of the architectural span of a work and the resources to put across his conception to the musicians. He was, through his study of the orchestral parts, alive to any difficulties the orchestra might encounter. They might have to make a quick turnover at a crucial passage or the parts being used might have become encrusted with markings, obliterating notes. Once at rehearsal he was asked about a particular note and, momentarily stumped for a reply, he consulted the score — held of course inches from his nose — duly giving the answer. Pausing, he then continued: "You must be very careful, I have seen your music and the part is not very good. It is rather old, and your turnover must be very quick there. You must take care." Nothing under Cantelli was ever left to chance, he was meticulous in every detail.

At the designated rehearsal time, Cantelli would walk to the podium only if there was complete silence. He would insist on total silence before coming on stage. On many occasions at the Festival Hall, he would send out Owen Mase in advance with instructions for Manoug Parikian to quieten the orchestra. Invariably he came dressed in a beautiful conducting jacket with a silken texture. He always looked immaculate, and never made concessions to an early hour. Musically too, there were no concessions at a Cantelli rehearsal and he expected the orchestra to give him its absolute attention; he expected to receive as much as he gave, no one was allowed to take the attitude that "it'll be all right on the night."

Standing on the podium, Guido appeared to take a mental roll-call. He was actually checking that players were seated where he expected to find them; it disconcerted him, when he looked for a player, to see him not in his position or missing, as was frequently the case with Dennis Brain. When Dennis took leave of absence for a solo engagement the entire horn section moved up one place and a replacement fourth horn was brought in. Cantelli would immediately spot this and ask Alfred Cursue (1949/60) the orchestra's fourth horn, to move back from third desk to fourth.

Cantelli then got down to the business of creating a performance. In his first rehearsals with the Philharmonia he would stop every few bars and give explanations as to what he required. As he grew to know the orchestra he realised that this was not the way to make music, that rehearsing in two- and four-bar phrases did not create the organic unity he sought. By letting the orchestra play, confident that each musician felt safe under his baton and trusted him implicity, he began to get the results he desired.

Guido told the orchestra, to follow his movements or, as it came out in his poor English: "follow my gesture." These movements were expressive and eloquent, emphasised by the very long baton. In contrast to Toscanini, whose beat was extremely economical, Cantelli's covered a much greater expanse and his whole body moved as if about to take off, his feet hardly seeming to touch the podium. "It was all done so gracefully, and so in time with the music. There was no movement which was in any way awkward, gauche or meaningless. That's another thing; all his movements meant something and he lived the music. He was more like a ballet dancer on the rostrum, I say that in the best possible spirit, not of criticism, but of admiration ... he had very good balance,and used his arms and hands very expressively — huge hands, you know, with very long fingers." (Manoug Parikian)

Before starting a work — and this was most conspicuous in the formal surroundings of a concert — Guido would be seen by the orchestra minutely arranging his feet so that they were together, with the tips of his toes just overlapping the front edge of the podium. As he did this he gave the impression of adjusting some internal balance until its pointer registered the correct position and he could begin the performance. To the audience, it often appeared as if Cantelli was standing on the podium — seemingly forever — waiting for the exact moment of inspiration.

Cellist Norina Semino (1950/60) was the only Italian in the Philharmonia and it fell to her to act as Cantelli's interpreter, translating back and forth from Italian to English to Italian. For her, Cantelli's gestures were but a means to an end: "There was no difficulty in understanding him and following him ... It's a question of that particular movement, that particular way of conducting. As Cantelli said, 'follow my gesture,' it isn't gesture, that's only a thing they have in their hand to express what comes from the heart — and it is from the heart. At the rehearsal, Cantelli never saved himself, it was like a performance always."

Before joining the Philharmonia, Norina Semino had not previously worked regularly in an orchestra, having devoted her career to solo work and chamber groups — she took part in many of the legendary wartime concerts organised by Myra Hess at the National Gallery, Early in her career in Italy, Norina had auditioned for Toscanini, in the hope that he would recommend her to concert agents. He liked her playing and wrote a brief note of introduction — which she still keeps. Years later, when the Maestro came to the Philharmonia, on learning that Norina was a member he asked to see her. "You do remember me, don't you,'" he touchingly enquired. Heart trouble brought Norina's career to a premature close in the late fifties. She was stricken by an attack during Otto Klemperer's recording sessions on the Mendelssohn *Italian* Symphony, during which she remained silent, despite considerable pain, rather than destroy the take.

Cantelli was extremely self-critical and would blame himself if he thought an interpretation failed to get across. After a while the orchestra learned to tell when these thoughts were running through Guido's mind. Gradually, while conducting a passage he would begin to look at his right forearm and a scowling, frowning look would come over his face. "It comes this morning, it comes not easy," he would be heard saying under his breath, and once, so disgusted by what he had done, he reeled against the podium rails panting, almost on the verge of fainting. Perhaps a few words of Italian escaped his lips for, instantly Norina put down her cello and rushed off stage leaving Guido looking for all the world like a lost child in front of the orchestra. Making her way to one of the Festival Hall bars, she asked the barman for a brandy, which he at first refused to serve as it was out of opening hours, only relenting when she explained that it was for the Maestro, for medicinal purposes. Guido received the brandy gratefully, swigging back the glass in one go to a chorus of "Cheers Maestro" and "Viva" from the orchestra. This provoked the comment from Cantelli that the Philharmonia was to him like a beautiful glass of water, but now he was going to fill it full with beautiful wine, instead of water!

There were always occasions during rehearsal when a musician would enter into discussions with Cantelli. No one ever deliberately asked a question to test his knowledge of a work but, if a contentious point did arise, questions were asked in the hope of clarifying what he had in mind. Sometimes arguments took place and Cantelli never gave way; knowing what he wanted, he would crucify the player concerned until a phrase was performed the way he required.

Neill Sanders (1950/57), the orchestra's second horn recalled: "He would drive the orchestra enormously hard, and he would always drive himself equally hard or harder. Most of the upsets and tantrums were really exasperations with himself, because he couldn't get what he wanted. If it was a matter of an individual solo from a player, he would drive the player until he got what he wanted, but then, he would have complete faith in the player, which is the marvellous thing about Cantelli."

There were players who could not take this kind of direction and they left the orchestra, to Guido's dismay, as when he returned for another season, he would ask in vain for the player who produced such a beautiful sound last time. After a demanding stretch of rehearsal, Guido sensed traces of animosity towards him from certain quarters, "They say I am too young," musicians close to him would hear him say, as if thinking aloud "Well, I am not too young to know what I know, and I will have what I want."

One brass player, out of sympathy with Cantelli, was put through twenty minutes of sheer hell and finally, heartily sick of it, turned on Cantelli saying sarcastically, "If you think you can do better, I'll lend you my instrument!" Not in the slightest caught out by this barbed question, Guido responded "Ah, yes, perhaps I would, but not today my lip is not in a good condition. I have not been able to practice," — going on to reminisce about his father's band and to display his vast technical knowledge of brass instruments.

When he came to record the Brahms First Symphony at Kingsway Hall in 1953, Cantelli was very taken by the sound of the trombone as used by the orchestra's new principal Alfred Flaszynski (1953/63). As Alfred Flaszynski recalled, he was invited by Cantelli to the conductor's room: "He was interested in what type of instrument I was using. In fact it was a German instrument, made in Hamburg. Apart from the horns, it was the only German brass instrument in the Philharmonia, because they all used American trumpets and trombones. When we recorded the Brahms First, he said, 'I like the sound so much, it is so suitable for Brahms.' I told him it was a German instrument, and he was quite interested to have this instrument imported to America. He wanted them to use this type of instrument — which of course the Americans would refuse."

As far as anyone can remember Cantelli was only wrong once on a musical point. Asking the orchestra to begin at a certain rehearsal figure, he gave a down beat, and immediately pulled them up. He repeated the instructions, again stopping the orchestra as soon as the began playing. This time he could be seen visibly tensing and trying not to lose his temper. Some of the musicians said they were playing from the correct number and that he must be wrong. Guido refused to believe them and again gave a downbeat — with the same result. Feeling that his authority was being challenged he rushed off stage, only to return soon after to concede defeat, having consulted the score and found himself to be at fault.

Cantelli rehearsals were conducted under enormous tension. This he could sustain for a full three hours but not always his musicians. They joked among themselves to lower the tension during the odd pauses which occur in most rehearsals. Cantelli rarely punctured the atmosphere he had so carefully built up. Once, after taking the orchestra through a passage several times, he brought them to a halt and someone let a note continue and die away. Clutching himself, as if embarrassed by the player's slight indiscretion, Guido cried, "Oh! no, no, no, you have wounded my prude." This caused rather a lot of laughter, as he had of course meant to say, "you have wounded my pride," but apart from the "prude," Guido's "wounded," had emerged as in "wind," a joke even he appreciated. A similiar occurrence had very different repercussions.

An overture by Rossini was being rehearsed. As Cantelli stopped the orchestra to explain something, Gareth Morris finished off the phrase with a "pom-pp-pom-pom-pom-pom" flourish. Immediately, Cantelli lashed into Morris, "Why do you make that sound? Why? Why? What is that?" and, working himself up to a formidable rage, continued, "You insult the composer by making that sound, you insulted the composer. Rossini is Italian national composer, it is national Italian music, you insult the entire Italian nation!!" Morris had used the music for his little joke, which was something Cantelli would not tolerate for, to him the score was holy writ and to do this, above all with an Italian work, was tantamount to showing a red rag to a bull. It was a very fraught moment, perhaps the worst in Cantelli's association with the orchestra.

"I regarded him as a neurotic person, he was in such a state about it all. He might have grown up, I found him underdeveloped. Although I was the same age as he was, no doubt I was underdeveloped — probably still am — but you can still observe can't you? Other people I compared him to, conductors I considered to be really great artists, and I don't think he was one. I think it was all pretty fast, and it was electric all the time ... the air was not one of relaxation. I did not enjoy playing for Cantelli, because there was never an atmosphere of enjoyment, to play the music and enjoy it, because he was always in a state himself." (Gareth Morris)

Despite these feelings, Gareth Morris still found he could respect Cantelli as a musician: "He was not a showman, but a genuine and very sincere musician, I'm sure of that." As far as Guido was concerned, the name "Morris" was anathema: he even declined an invitation to go for a spin in a musician's new car because it was a Morris!

As Cantelli brought his rehearsal to an end, he would say to the orchestra, "Tonight, give me everything you've got." Coming as it did after a rehearsal in which they had done just that, he was asking a great deal. But as violist Leo Birnbaum (1947/58) remarked, "If a conductor is able to hold the interest of an orchestra for several rehearsals before the concert, he will almost certainly get a great performance. This Cantelli was always able to do."

Following a Festival Hall rehearsal, there occurred Guido Cantelli's one and only meeting with Sir Thomas Beecham. Until the hall was completed in the mid-Sixties and the artist's entrance re-sited, the huge instrument lift doubled as a passenger lift serving the artist's entrance. As Guido approached the lift to descend, he joined several of the orchestra's principals, and one or two other musicians in conversation. As they entered, a back-desk violinist slipped into the lift virtually unnoticed. Somewhat overawed by such close proximity to his young Maestro, the musician went to the farthest corner and tried to make himself as inconspicuous as possible — which his small stature, combined with the great size of the lift made relatively easy. Reaching ground level, the jaw-like doors parted to reveal Sir Thomas, arriving for a rehearsal with his Royal Philharmonic Orchestra, accompanied by a member of the hall's staff, who attempted to introduce the two conductors by saying, "Sir Thomas, let me introduce you to the young Italian Maestro Guido Cantelli ..." Beecham however, ignored him and, spotting the timid violinist — a former member of his orchestra — in the corner, lunged forward and shook him warmly by the hand.

*

Cantelli's 1954 Edinburgh Festival concerts with the Philharmonia marked his first appearance there since his British debut with the La Scala orchestra four years previously. In two consecutive reviews, "The Scotsman" said this of Cantelli:

> Cantelli conducts from memory. So do many other conductors, but actually he remembers what is in the score ... He accepts the music as it is and devotes his energies exclusively to the realisation of the composer's intentions. This is one of the reasons why he is a great and not a star conductor.
>
> Incredible though it may seem, Guido Cantelli, still in his early thirties may soon achieve that position of supremacy among conductors which was so long enjoyed by the now retired Toscanini ... they have much in common, though the young maestro has not yet the maturity and magisterial authority of Toscanini.

Cantelli returned to Edinburgh in 1955, leading the New York Philharmonic Symphony with whom he had undertaken a European tour. Under Cantelli they gave two concerts, with their remaining programmes at the festival being conducted by Dimitri Mitropoulos and George Szell. By now, Cantelli had a special affection for the Usher Hall, as he explained in his "Scotsman" Festival Diary interview: " ... there is such a live sound in this Hall, when we play in this Hall it is easy for us: everything comes out so well, so clearly."

The published festival programme announced that Cantelli's second concert would include a performance of Copland's Third Symphony but this did not take place. This omission was greeted with cries of disgust from the critics, who bitterly complained about the lack of any new American music in the orchestra's programmes. The Symphony never featured in any of Cantelli's programmes, although its optimistic outlook and Mahlerian dimensions made it an ideal work for a Cantelli interpretation. Very likely, the festival planners had confused this piece with the one work of Copland's that Cantelli did have in his repertoire, the ever popular *El Salón México*, which he did give at the festival. As "The Scotsman" reported, it was " ... played with crackling exuberence ... an exhilarating Fiesta."

*

Guido Cantelli made his debut with the New York Philharmonic Symphony Orchestra in January 1952. Of all the orchestras he worked with, Cantelli made more appearances with the Philharmonic Symphony that any other, partly, it must be admitted, because of their subscription season, which required each programme to be given up to four performances over the period Thursday to Sunday.

An aspect of the Philharmonic Symphony programmes which makes them unique in Cantelli's career is that he regularly appeared in these concerts accompanying concerto soloists. There were concerto performances at La Scala, but not on the scale we find here. These concerto performances were probably included more for the benefit of the New York audiences, who liked to have a big-name soloist, performing — preferably — one of the popular concertos, than because Cantelli had any desire to direct a concerto performance. It was normal Philharmonic Symphony programming which, like it or not, Cantelli had to fit in with. Collaborating in these performances brought Cantelli into contact with musicians such as Claudio Arrau, Wilhelm Backhaus, Robert Casadesus, Rudolf Firkušný, Walter Gieseking, Jascha Heifetz, Nicole Henriot-Schwitzer, Rudolf Serkin, Isaac Stern and László Varga.

Fascinating glimpses of what a Philharmonic Symphony concerto performance with Cantelli involved have come from Rudolf Firkušný and Isaac Stern. Stern only performed once with Cantelli, but Firkušný appeared intermittently with him throughout his career. In New York they performed concertos by Menotti, Dvořák, Beethoven and Brahms. A Mozart concerto was planned for December 1956, but Leonard Bernstein took over. Rudolf Firkšný described his first meeting with Cantelli, prior to their opening rehearsal:

We met shortly before the first rehearsal and Cantelli was always extremely well prepared, conducting most of the standard repertory from memory.

I enjoyed working with him enormously as we felt a certain affinity in our musical ideas; also, his scrupulous preparation of the orchestra made the collaboration quite ideal.

The performances had to go well after his careful preparation in rehearsals. Although he was demanding and young, he was greatly respected by the orchestra members and I think very much liked as a person.

Isaac Stern gave two performances of the *Symphonie Espagnole* by Lalo with Cantelli:

It would be difficult to forget them . . . just as we came together, meeting musically for the first time . . . Cantelli said to me, "Please be sure to indicate very clearly to me what you want because not only have I never conducted this work, I have never even heard it!" I looked at him in some astonishment as it was hard to conceive of any musician already in his early thirties who had not somehow, somewhere heard performances of this often-performed, standard repertoire work.

Within a few minutes of the beginning of the rehearsal, however, I realised that Mr. Cantelli was indeed telling the truth. He did not know the work and had no idea of the performance traditions or the necessary rubatos implicit in a representative performance of this virtuoso vehicle.

We worked very hard that day and the next, but I had to keep a very careful eye on his stick and he on me, as we played the performance and engaged in constant eye-to-eye communication to make certain that we did not slip away from each other in sudden opposite directions.

He was a quick study and gave everything he had into the performances. During one of them, he almost impaled his left hand with the baton with the passion of his final beat at the end of the first movement. No matter what he conducted, he immersed himself in the music and his total concentration resulted in a sort of blazing communication that augured well for his future. He was a music maker — not merely a time beater.

Firkušný observed Cantelli maturing over the seasons:

. . . I was amazed by his steady growth and maturing process. Our last performance . . . showed that his attitude towards the orchestra had mellowed somewhat, yet without any concessions in his demands.

Cantelli's stringent demands were bitterly resented by certain members of the orchestra, who told him outright that they would not take his kind of direction from anyone, least of all from a man of his age. They pointed out that they had crushed greater names than him — the orchestra was known as the 'conductor's graveyard' — and if need be, he too would receive the same treatment. Tempers on both sides reached boiling point, with Cantelli's instructions being flouted to such a degree by these musicians that rather than take any more insults, he walked out on the orchestra. This precipitated a confrontation between Cantelli, the musicians and the orchestra's management, who came out firmly behind their players. At some point in this argument, the musicians' union intervened, telling Cantelli to give way or they would prevent him from conducting in New York again.

Cantelli continued to receive invitations for seasons with the Philharmonic Symphony, yet for all the artistic triumphs he undoubtedly enjoyed with the orchestra, he was never happy in the way he was in London. For a man of Cantelli's sensibilities, the orchestra's schedule must have been killing, and did finally take its toll. When he failed to acknowledge the applause after a performance of the Brahms Third Symphony in Carnegie Hall on January 20, 1955, it was because he had collapsed in the wings as he came off stage. Press reports stated that Cantelli was suffering from a virus infection: in fact he had not eaten a proper meal in days; the orchestra was demanding so much of him that mundane things like food were forgotten in a virtual twenty-four hours a day preoccupation with music.

As each New York season drew to a close, Guido became like a schoolboy ticking off the days till end of term. He would leave both his and Iris's trunks in a prominent position in their hotel suite to remind him that it would not be long before they were to be packed and the time to be leaving would have arrived.

*

Guido Cantelli's recording career encompassed the final years of the 78, the early Mono LP's and the first experimental Stereophonic recordings. Cantelli was the first conductor of the generation making a career after the war to benefit from these technological advances. As such, one might have expected him to have taken a keen interest in all that was going on around him, but his attitude appears to have been one of almost total indifference. He made no artistic concessions to the medium, expecting it to make concessions to him so that he could concentrate on the one thing that mattered — the music.

Recording sessions with the Philharmonia were scheduled around his London seasons, with works drawn from current programmes. In selecting works for recording, Cantelli worked very closely with David Bicknell, who produced all his Philharmonia recordings. Cantelli never, however, used the concerts as a public rehearsal prior to a recording. For him the live experience of music was paramount, a recording was at best a substitute to be enjoyed in his absence. For someone who felt this way, recording created problems, as it was not possible to perform the music in the studio exactly as if at a concert. Recording demanded a re-interpretation of an interpretation, in terms of pure sound, a concept that Cantelli found very hard to grasp. He could not understand that the sound of a work as he had performed it in concert, was not reproduced when he listened to a play back. Orchestral balances needed to be re-thought and dynamics altered thus introducing for him musically alien difficulties. It is hardly suprising that Cantelli hated recording.

Recording sessions generally have a fairly relaxed atmosphere but this was not the case with Cantelli. As with his concert rehearsals, he would step on to the podium at Kingsway Hall — where the majority of his recordings were made after 1951 — expecting to be greeted by complete silence. If his concentration was broken by a musician talking, or last-minute tuning, he would instantly disappear into the conductor's room, and would only start the session when absolute silence had been established.

While Guido rehearsed the work to be recorded the engineers carried out their microphone level and balance checks. Eventually, Guido would announce that he was ready for a take, which for him meant a performance of a complete movement of a symphony or a complete shorter work, not a few bars which could be edited together with other short takes to form the whole. He refused to record in bits and pieces but sought to preserve on disc, a performance that had a genuine organic unity. Rarely did a first take suffice and, after hearing the play back, he would make any necessary adjustments before attempting another. This might result in a wrong note on an important solo, a fluffed entry or a lapse in ensemble, passable in the context of a live performance, but not suitable for repeated gramophone listening. Peering at his watch — à la Toscanini — Cantelli would say to the orchestra: "In one hour," or "In half an hour, we will give another performance." At which time another was given, and if after that mistakes still occured, or he felt some reason to be dissatisfied, the whole process was repeated, and repeated, until the perfection he desired was finally acheived. It is no wonder that members of the Philharmonia recall Cantelli's sessions taking longer than anyone else's; and they remember one above all which exemplifies the lengths to which Cantelli would go to get his living performance.

The 1952 season featured performances of Ravel's *Pavane pour une infante defunte* little more than a page of music. Cantelli must have liked the sound of this sombre little piece in the Festival Hall acoustic as it was here that the recording took place, a matter of weeks after the concert performances. The recording presented a wonderful opportunity for the engineers to test out the hall as a possible future recording venue and the sessions were almost certainly the first undertaken there.

Although it was a simple piece Cantelli went through take after take after take. Tension mounted and each fresh attempt became more nerve-racking until, finally Cantelli in frustration rushed off stage to the conductor's room. Renata Scheffel-Stein, the orchestra's principal harpist (1951/74), remembered going to see him there. "Can't you understand, I lost my nephew," she recalls him saying: "I lost my nephew, when I play this piece, I always see my nephew." Guido had been deeply attached to his nephew Sergio (the brother of Mariangela) whose death in November 1951, aged 12, left him with a profound sense of grief. To express his love for Sergio, Guido promised to dedicate his next performance of the *Pavane* to his memory, and the work appears in an NBC Symphony programme that December. Now as he tried to record the work his close involvement in the music brought back cherished images of Sergio, which may go some way towards explaining his extraordinary behaviour.

The harp always created insuperable difficulties for Cantelli at recording sessions, nowhere more so than on this recording, as he could not find a way of balancing it correctly in the orchestral texture. Renata Scheffel-Stein remembered that: "He was always shouting, arrrrp! arrrrp! just like a dog. Always shouting before the harp even started to play." This session left her in tears, and later induced a pathological state of fear whenever Cantelli came to direct the orchestra.

Whatever mental torments Renata Scheffel-Stein endured over this work, they were nothing compared to the sheer physical effort required from Dennis Brain, whose taxing horn solo became infinitely more demanding when he was asked to repeat it over and over again. This solo, one of the longest for the horn ever written, lasting as it does virtually the entire work, was not the cause of Cantelli's difficulties, purely his inability to balance the harp. Neill Sanders witnessed what Dennis Brain was going through:

I thought it was going on forever. For Dennis Brian it was an enormous challenge, and he took it as a challenge. This was the interesting thing, because after you'd done it three or four times, you think: that's it, now surely they've got it. By then he was playing beautifully, but it just went on and on, and on. This certainly made life difficult, for us in a less responsible position, because suddenly the responsibility of your own part became enormous, at the thought of mucking it up for the other man. So that it became quite nerve-racking for the rest of us after the umpteenth take.

I can remember Cantelli, just about to start. He put down his baton, looked at Dennis and said, 'If I could only give you my lungs.' But Dennis in a way was enjoying himself, no matter how many times he'd do it, it was just as beautiful each time.

Nevertheless, Dennis felt that he had to say something, and made his feelings known to Manoug Parikan, who recalled:

Cantelli was so insistent on every detail being right, I fear he put too much strain on the orchestra, and certainly on Dennis Brain. After a time, repetition becomes stale, and Dennis was the exact opposite of Cantelli, he was the natural musician who played things quite naturally without thinking about them.

We did something like seventeen or eighteen takes and by that time Dennis did come and complain to me. 'My lips are cracking up, I don't think I can go on playing,' he said. Which of course was absolutely true. I think that was a lack of judgement on the part of Cantelli or, lack of experience if you like, not realising that one player, even of the incredible calibre of Dennis Brain, could not go on producing the same peak results.

The seventeen or eighteen takes remembered by Manoug Parikian were no exaggeration, other musicians have recollections of around twenty being made before Cantelli was finally satisfied. Out of this came a performance which, to the innocent ear, captures the very essence of an inspiration caught on its first wing. Only when the listener is aware of what those five minutes and fifty seconds cost does the atmosphere surrounding them become tangible. A barely perceptible hesitation before an important orchestral solo; noises as players tense themselves in their chairs; above all, there is discernible the feeling that at any moment Cantelli will call a halt to the proceedings.

Other works cost as much effort: twenty takes were expended on Debussy's *Nocturnes*, although the famous passage for muted trumpets in *Fêtes* which might have been written for Cantelli to agonise over — passed off without incident. He did not require any special mutes, or resort to unusual orchestral positioning. It is a pity that he did not record the third piece *Sirènes*, with its hauntingly beautiful sounds, from the wordless female choir. He never included *Sirènes* in any of his concert performances of the *Nocturnes*, so perhaps he failed to come under its spell (The Philharmonia recorded the complete set under Carlo Maria Giulini, and later as the New Philharmonia under Pierre Boulez.)

Between takes on *Daphnis et Chloé*, Cantelli returned constantly to the score, as if trying to find something which had eluded him at the previous attempt. This recording took so long, that it had to be split over two of his London seasons. Nothing came easy at these sessions with Cantelli; everyone worked under phenomenal pressure, the slightest matter of detail being enough to break Cantelli's train of thought. He literally cried over Schumann's Fourth Symphony, when a playback sounded completely different to what he had heard the orchestra produce in the hall. At the other extreme, when a flock of starlings landed on the roof of Kingsway Hall and ruined a take with their chattering, he laughed out loud! There is also one legacy of Cantelli's sessions at the hall that remains to this day, as a reminder to members of the Philharmonia of one of the most ecstatic musical experiences of their lives.

In his incidental music for Gabriele D'Annunzio's mystical play, *Le Martyre de Saint-Sébastien*, composed in 1911, Debussy aimed at creating a work that broke new ground musically, at the same time harking back to earlier musical forms. What emerged, was a lack-lustre, tired-sounding work, that André Caplet arranged for orchestra without the vocal parts as four "Fragments Symphoniques," first heard in Paris, in 1912. They were brought to London, by Ernest Ansermet, in January 1929 and Cantelli had performed them seven times before putting his interpretation on disc.

Conductor and record producer Charles Gerhardt sat in at these sessions: "I'll never forget him balancing the six horns . . . my hair stood on end, and he didn't get past the first page as I remember for about forty-five minutes. What I remember was his total knowledge of that very difficult score, and I doubt that he ever looked at the music or turned a page, but he was going on about balances, and about chords. Certain wind would play chords, and the horns, and so on. He stopped, and he would say, 'the D natural, a little quieter,' and then they'd play it again, and then, 'the B flat, a little louder,' and suddenly he'd say: 'The whole chord like this,' and you got goose pimples . . . the first forty-five minutes went by and the strings hadn't played a note, they were fascinated, they were like they went to a Saturday-night thriller movie, they ate it up. In most people's rehearsals there's nothing more boring than when you're not playing and the conductor is working with another section; Guido was one of those possessed conductors who was so inevitably right about what he was doing, that it was fascinating watching him at work. He never wasted anybody's time . . . but with this piece, it just took a long time . . ."

"To a lot of people, it's a throwaway piece. This was made out to be the greatest work ever written — but then Cantelli played every work as the greatest ever written. I can still remember the wonderful sounds of the orchestra, it sounded like a gigantic organ . . ." (Clem Relf)

Violinist Hans Geiger (1949/62), thought it: "One of the most beautiful sounds my ears have ever experienced. It was absolutely fantastic, breathtaking!"

At the completion of a take, everyone in Kingsway Hall was in a state of excitement, knowing that something unique had been caught. Cantelli, his face beaming with the knowledge that he had got what he wanted, stayed on the podium, as his recording team entered the hall offering their congratulations — dropping at the same time a veritable bombshell! It would have to be re-recorded; there were too many studio noises.

Musicians at Kingsway Hall used bent wood chairs which had over the years dried out, making them liable to creak and groan, as the musicians moved while playing their instruments. In a quiet passage these creaks and groans were picked up by the microphones, and indeed, there are several very distinct "studio noises" present on the *Sébastien* recording which was released (suggesting that Cantelli did not in fact re-record these movements). Guido was brought down to earth with a bang and made his feelings clear to the engineers: "We have been playing the most wonderful music; this is a beautiful orchestra; we have played so beautifully, and now you come and tell me that. Whose fault it is? Nobody but yours. You are responsible. I come not again to record, until my musicians have iron chairs!" Cantelli flatly refused to continue and the session broke up. When the orchestra assembled to complete the recording a few days later, two furniture vans were parked outside the hall. Steel-framed chairs were being taken inside: the same steel-framed chairs in use today. Cantelli's iron chairs!

*

There were four concerts in Cantelli's 1955 London season and, for the first time, there were empty seats at some concerts. This was not a reflection on his performances, but rather his predilection for repeating works from one concert to another. With so few appearences each season, audiences perhaps felt that Cantelli was not offering them enough music and the inclusion of a concerto might have dispelled that impression.

He could only manage one London engagement in 1956, and this was for two performances of the Verdi *Requiem*, on July 1 and 6. Arriving in late May, Cantelli began a series of intensive recording sessions. *Daphnis et Chloë* was completed, and this cleared the decks for recordings of two Beethoven symphonies, the Seventh, to be followed by the Fifth.

At one of these sessions, Cantelli sat alone at the back of Kingsway Hall, while the orchestra filed out for a break. (He seldom ate at rehearsals or sessions.) Violist Bernard Davis (1945/68) had also stayed behind and thought Cantelli was checking points in the score until the Maestro looked up and motioned him to come over. There was no score in sight, Guido had before him a collection of family photographs. Handing them over, Cantelli remarked: "After my next engagements, there will be no more flying, no more touring, I will stay in Milan, and concentrate on my work at La Scala."

It was through Bernard Davis that this biography came about. Three years after Cantelli's death, I received from him as a birthday present, Cantelli's recording of *Romeo and Juliet*. At thirteen, I was just starting to explore music through records, but attending concerts was something I had yet to experience. The name Guido Cantelli meant nothing to me: whereas the words Philharmonia and Royal Festival Hall were just coming into my consciousness. As a long-standing family friend, Bernard would often call in and see us — usually on the way to a session at Abbey Road. Sensing my growing interest in music, he caught me at exactly the right moment for an introduction to Cantelli. Presenting me with the record, I recall him saying: "This conductor Guido Cantelli, was killed in a plane crash at the age of thirty-six. Had he lived he would have become the world's greatest conductor." When someone makes a statement like that to a thirteen year old, it certainly makes an impression: heightened by listening to the Tchaikovsky, which bowled me over. The music alone caused this reaction, as it was new to me, only as I grew to know Cantelli's interpretation and compare it to others, did the greatness of his vision, sweep all others aside. (Cantelli felt this work so deeply, that he could not restrain himself from telling the orchestra during a rehearsal of the finale, "Oh, this is so sad!") From this has come a lifelong interest in the art of Guido Cantelli, and a profound regret, that I was too young ever to have experienced that art in person.

Cantelli began work on Beethoven's Fifth Symphony. At the first session he took the orchestra through a complete performance, a year having passed since they had last performed the work together. Tragically, this run-through was not taped by the engineers, for fate, evoked in the opening bars of the symphony, was to decree that Cantelli left this recording unfinished.

All went well until a take was ruined by a thunderous noise, eventually traced to a delivery of coal being made to the Kingsway Hall boiler room. When Cantelli heard of this he shrugged his shoulders philosophically, remarking that, neither he nor the orchestra would like to play in a cold, unheated building. Worse was to come. Directly behind Kingsway Hall are the Connaught Rooms, a huge set of banqueting suites, at the time undergoing a major reconstruction, and building noise percolated through into the hall. At considerable expense EMI came to an arrangement with the building contractors, whereby each time the red light came on, they would cease work for the duration. Under these conditions, the first, second and part of the third movements were recorded. Noise somehow still filtered through, however, and no matter how Guido tried to fight it, he could not achieve the complete concentration he required and without warning he brought the session to a close. As the musicians were putting their instruments away, one of them approached Cantelli proferring a small hammer — the type used for tacks. Originally he had planned to present it to Cantelli on completion of the recording, as a token of the Maestro's triumph over the noise created by the builders next door: a noise that, as it turned out, not even Beethoven and Cantelli could drown. Realising what this gesture meant, Guido seized on the hammer and brandished it high above his head. An enormous smile crossed his face and he laughed out loud, as if to say that, while he was defeated on this occasion, things would be different next time and that he, like the motto in Beethoven's Fifth, would return in triumph.

Everyone felt a keen sense of frustration, but Cantelli reassured David Bicknell that he would be able to stop over between engagements in the autumn and complete the recording when, hopefully, work on the Connaught would have finished. What remained of the sessions allocated to the Beethoven, were transferred to Abbey Road where Guido recorded Mozart's Twenty-Ninth Symphony — the only work he recorded with the orchestra, which had never performed in public with them. In the circumstances it was a fitting choice, as the music perfectly expressed, in his performance, all that he felt within himself at that moment.

It did not take long for the orchestra to notice that, on this occasion, Guido had come to London without Iris. He soon explained that she was pregnant and that the birth was expected during his current season with the orchestra. The Cantellis had long wanted to start a family and, when one looked like not occuring naturally had even taken the step of consulting doctors. By now, such was the bond of friendship that had grown up between Cantelli and the Philharmonia that his news aroused great interest among the players. Suddenly, Guido's family had acquired another ninety members who all felt they were part of the forthcoming happy event! Throughout, he kept in touch with Milan and returned to Via Livorno in time for the birth of Leonardo Guido on June 10. When the Philharmonia assembled for a session a couple of days later, David Bicknell read out a telegram from Guido announcing the birth, news which was greeted with much jubilation.

*

The impresario S.A. Gorlinsky was quoted in the music press as saying that the two performances of the Verdi *Requiem* were going to cost

£5,000 and full houses were needed to break even. For these performances, the orchestra were joined by the Croydon Philharmonic Choir (the Philharmonia Chorus was not formed until 1957). Before all the forces came together, orchestral rehearsals were held, at which Guido astounded the orchestra by singing all the solo parts, not just filling in the vocal lines by way of accompaniment to the orchestra, but with real under-standing: an understanding for Verdi's work, that transmitted itself to the audience in the Festival Hall. As the hushed coda receded into silence, a wave of people — many with tears streaming down their faces — surged towards the platform, to shout their appreciation to the artists, in particular Cantelli, whose interpretation was summed up in one word by Clem Relf: "Shattering."

No one present at the performances of the Verdi *Requiem* could have dreamt they were the last Cantelli would ever give at the Festival Hall and the last occasion he would conduct the Philharmonia. Future plans involved him in even greater ties with the orchestra, and he was being given *carte-blanche* over his choice of programme material. "Guido was in love with the Philharmonia of London. If he could, he would stay with the Philharmonia from the First of January, to the Thirty-First of December — all the time — morning, afternoon and night-time. He was really in love, as much as a man can love a woman, he loved the Philharmonia." (Iris Cantelli)

Those last weeks saw Cantelli's personal relationships with members of the orchestra move on to an entirely different plane. All the tensions which so often surrounded him seemed to dissolve and what had previously cost great personal effort came easily. As he sat talking with the musicians in a few spare moments at rehearsal his great love of football emerged. This provoked a lively discussion, in the course of which Manoug Parikian and Clem Relf announced that they were fervent supporters of Arsenal and attended home matches at Highbury whenever the orchestra's schedule allowed. Guido's face lit up at the mention of Arsenal because, outside Novara, they were his favourite side, and he immediately made them promise to take him to a match when he returned in the autumn.

For the musicians of the Philharmonia Cantelli's death took with it a part of their lives.

> It seemed like almost the end of the world for a day or so. It was very difficult to accept, the whole orchestra was absolutely shaken rigid by it, just like a family loss. (Clem Relf)
>
> I remember finding it difficult to believe at all, because it was so dreadful . . . that such a thing could happen. He was very special. (Jean Lefevre)
>
> I came home, and I was crying like mad. My husband said to me, 'Are you crazy, he treated you so badly, aren't you glad that he's gone?' I said no, terrible, terrible, terrible. You know, I just couldn't get over it, that he died so early. (Renata Scheffel-Stein)

I think the world is a far poorer place without the likes of Cantelli. We have something from him that is precious; that he's inspired us both in our lives, and in the making of music. We shan't see the like of him again. (Arthur Davison)

I was stunned, I couldn't believe it. I couldn't accept it for a long time. There was a void — a complete emptiness — it took some time to get used to the idea that he had gone. (Norina Semino)

As time went on and we worked more and more with him, one really looked forward to the sessions. You knew that occasionally there would be outbursts of temperament, which livened up the proceedings — although it might be your turn to get a rocket. You knew that you were going to get down to some really enjoyable music-making, with a splendid musician. I always think his idea of a performance was perfection, or as near perfection as you could get. One of his sayings which I still remember was that you would play something at a rehearsal or session and after a few moments silence he would say, 'Yes it was good, but good is not marvellous, next time it will be marvellous.' And to make it marvellous, he spared neither himself, nor the orchestra. (Cecil James, principal Bassoon 1950/64)

*

Returning to Italy, Guido spent a few weeks holiday with Iris and Leonardo at "Genzianella Alpino" before taking up rehearsals at Piccola Scala, prior to the company's forthcoming performances at the Johannesburg Festival, which featured his own production of Mozart's *Così fan tutte*, the only opera Guido conducted at Teatro alla Scala.

*

Toscanini may have planted the seed which resulted in Dr. Ghiringhelli announcing that La Scala were contemplating building a small auditorium, next to the main theatre, for operatic productions of a more intimate character, unsuitable for the main theatre's huge stage.

Toscanini's 1950 NBC broadcast of Verdi's *Falstaff*, had kindled in him one last great musical dream: to conduct *Falstaff* in a small theatre, as the composer originally intended. *Falstaff* runs like a thread throughout Toscanini's career, as if he was reborn artistically each time he conducted the work. Only twice in his association with *Falstaff*, which began with performances at La Scala in 1898, had Toscanini fully realised Verdi's intentions and given the opera in a small theatre. Both of these performances had taken place at Busseto, the town where Carlo Verdi had registered the birth of his son Joseph — known as Giuseppe — in 1813. Toscanini had given a centenary performance there, and later another to mark the twenty-fifth anniversary of Verdi's death. 1951 presented a wonderful opportunity for a fiftieth anniversary production, but it was not to be. As Piccola Scala took shape Toscanini saw that it had the potential to fulfil his dream and he persuaded Dr. Ghiringhelli that only he could conduct the opening performance — which had to be *Falstaff.*

Luchino Visconti was selected as producer and Toscanini insisted that he should aim at a new visualisation. Toscanini also wanted his production to act as a vehicle for the many young singers whose careers were just starting. For Toscanini these performances had acquired a double significance: they would certainly be the last he would conduct at La Scala, and they were his personal valediction to the composer he had served all his life. Even the events of April 1954 did nothing to subdue his enthusiasm, and he was back in Milan that summer confident of returning the following year for the *première.* Unfortunately, however, once back in New York his health declined and his dream was finally snuffed out forever when his doctors forbade him to conduct again.

Concurrently with Toscanini's preparations on *Falstaff,* Piccola Scala were laying plans for their subsequent productions, including *Così fan tutte* under Cantelli. When Toscanini told Dr. Ghiringhelli of his enforced retirement, he suggested that Cantelli be given the opening performances. Mozart's opera was almost unknown at La Scala, where it had not received a performance for over thirty years. The two-hundredth anniversary of the composer's death fell on January 27, 1956 and with the dropping of *Falstaff* this date presented itself as the most suitable for the opening of the new theatre. Of course, Cantelli did not choose this opera for that reason alone, as Luigi Alva, who took the role of Ferrando, commented: "I think Maestro Cantelli chose this particular piece because it is really a masterpiece, and he liked very much the mathematical feeling of this opera, in which everything is perfect — has to be symmetric. I think he liked the intimate atmosphere in which to work, almost by hand."

Maestro Picozzi, a teacher at the Scuola di Canto at La Scala, was assigned as producer, but he retired after a few days because of an artistic difference with Cantelli. Faced with his defection, Cantelli made the decision to become his own producer. In the past, in all the operatic productions with which he had been connected, he had only been musical director, with the artistic concept in other hands. Now the opportunity was before him to achieve what he long wanted to attempt: the total fusion between stage action and music which could only take place if the entire concept came from one guiding hand. Because of his lack of stage experience, Guido was offered several different producers but elected to work with only a stage manager to advise on technical matters. Cantelli's production was not revolutionary — in fact it was rather old fashioned, but the inspiration was entirely drawn from the music. It is difficult to discover exactly how long Cantelli had studied the score prior to the first rehearsals — he obviously knew the work some time in advance, as we shall see— but a considerable length of time was involved, probably stretching over a number of years. Once work began, Iris Cantelli remembered Guido saying, "Now I am prepared to conduct opera."

Cantelli's well-chosen cast, was a blend of youthful experience with youthful inexperience: Elisabeth Schwarzkopf (Fiordiligi), Nan Merriman (Dorabella), Graziella Sciutti (Despina), Rolando Panerai (Guglielmo), Luigi Alva (Fernando) and Franco Calabrese (Don Alfonso). Schwarzkopf was portraying Fiordiligi on stage for the first time although, together with Nan Merriman and Rolando Panerai, she had taken part in Karajan's Philharmonia recording of the opera. Luigi Alva, Franco Calabrese and Graziella Sciutti were all taking roles in Cimarosa's *Il matrimonio segreto*, which went into production at Piccola Scala, under Giorgio Strehler, at the same time as Cantelli's *Così*. This led to considerable backstage confusion as singers commuted between productions, and the management dithered over which production should open the theatre, eventually deciding on the Cimarosa, which opened on December 26, 1956, conducted by Nino Sanzogno.

The length of time Cantelli had spent preparing *Così fan tutte* can be judged by the fact that Luigi Alva auditioned for the role of Ferrando two years before the opera was performed. He was then still a student at La Scala's opera school, and received one month's notice to prepare the aria: "Un aura amorosa.' Like everyone, he knew that a production of *Così* was in the offing, but as yet he did not have any of its music in his repertoire. Unable to afford the complete score, Alva purchased the aria — just four pages — from Casa Ricordi — "Cost less you know!" — and set about preparing for his audition.

Cantelli, de Sabata, and Dr. Ghiringhelli, together with other important members of the music staff of La Scala, were sitting in the main auditorium, assessing the vocal talent being presented. This was a line-up calculated to induce feelings of apprehension in any young singer, but not Luigi Alva:

Waiting for my turn, I have to say I was not nervous, because I heard some people before me, and I got some confidence, because I thought I was going to be better. 'Mr. Alva, it is your turn.' The pianist started, and right away Maestro Cantelli says, 'Excuse me, in what key are you singing?' In that moment we realised that my edition was printed one tone down. My goodness, it means changing all the preparation.

I started to sing a sort of improvisation, suddenly, I saw this small man coming towards the stage with interest, and that gave me more courage. He stopped me and says, 'Would you please repeat again the same phrase,' and I repeat. 'Now you make *piano* this phrase.' He started to conduct a little, then interrupted again, and ran to meet the other people in the group. They were talking and at that moment I realised that maybe he [Cantelli] was interested in my performance.

Several months before rehearsals began, Cantelli assembled his cast, in order to explain his visualisation of the production and to give him the opportunity to meet the singers informally and get to know them in person. They would be spending a lot of time in each other's company over the coming weeks and if there were to be any artistic differences now was the time to part, rather than later, when any disruption could upset the entire balance of the production. Of all operas, *Così fan tutte* depends on ensemble, and Cantelli wanted a true ensemble, not six individual personalities unaffected by the actions on stage.

He organised a series of one-hour coaching sessions, in which each singer received tuition in his or her role. A typical schedule for these read:

> 1400 hrs — Elisabeth Schwarzkopf.
> 1500 hrs — Graziella Sciutti.
> 1600 hrs — Nan Merriman.

and so on.

"I knocked on the door. There was a half-chord piano — not a grand piano — and this elegant man in grey making some arpeggios on the piano, no score at all in front of him. He started to make an atmosphere that absolutely frightened me.". This was how Luigi Alva described his first session with Cantelli. After passing the time of day, the man in grey at the piano continued by saying:

> Well Alva, you know when I chose my cast . . . I thought of you, because you have all the qualities to make a good Ferrando. For me this is very important because it is the first opera I will conduct in this house, and it is a big responsibility for me. I don't say this to make you afraid — no, you can do perfectly all right . . . This is why you have to give me not one hundred per cent, I don't ask for one hundred, but two hundred.

A casual encounter with one of his singers during routine business at La Scala, would bring forth a stream of questions from Guido relating to their role. He would ask about specific interpretative points, how they were dealing with them, give his views, and expect them to have mastered any technical problems by the time of the next rehearsal. There were countless rehearsals — Iris Cantelli recalls a total of eighty! Whatever the exact number, the cast found themselves living in the theatre, morning, noon and night.

It was Graziella Sciutti's first performance of the impish maid Despina. Her success in this production led to her making the role very much her own, and she took it to most of the world's leading opera houses, by way of Salzburg, and a decade of performances under Karl Böhm. Graziella described Cantelli's approach to them:

> When Guido arrived for the first rehearsal, he knew the score upside down, he knew everything he wanted. He allowed us to discuss, very seldom he

accepted, the discussion finished saying he was right! But, there was a possibility of discussion. Every afternoon, we had at least two or three hours — if not more — of only recitatives, with Guido Cantelli at the piano, sitting and discussing them. That was the most interesting work, which we never got tired of.

Working in such close proximity to his singers, each of whom had assumed the mask of the personality they were interpreting, made Guido more aware than before of the real people behind their stage personas. As they grew to know him, their empathy became a two-way transmission, with Guido giving more of himself, in the presence of people he knew he could trust. "At the beginning, he wasn't so keen getting into our group, and way of thinking. Joking was never allowed from the beginning of rehearsal, not even after rehearsal, everything was very serious. After a month or so, he started laughing with us, and we discovered actually a very warm heart in him, that we hadn't suspected in the beginning." (Graziella Sciutti)

Cantelli was in effect living *Così fan tutte*, his whole being, mental and physical, was given over to Mozart. Unlike a concert work a three-hour rehearsal of which produced a recognizable performance, *Così fan tutte* emerged from rehearsal number by number, with these being attached to their accompanying stage actions, like a huge jig-saw being slotted together over a wide time-span. Cantelli's problem, was that he could not see an overall picture, although the score was there complete in his mind it was being broken up in front of him and it nagged at him that it might not fit back together as he had conceived. "Guido got really very nervous when he prepared *Così fan tutte*. He probably couldn't see, day by day, the quality of the performance getting better and better. It is the only situation I can remember, when Guido didn't face a conducting problem with completely cold blood." (Giuseppe Gallini)

Cantelli did not take the subtitle "Comic Opera" at face value, to him the work went far deeper: "He didn't see a comedy, and in that I agree with him entirely. It's not a tragedy, but it's not the opera buffa it's often taken for. He took things very seriously, and it's a very bitter opera in a way . . . the situation would develop to be funny, but the character who was performing didn't do a little trick to make the people laugh. That is where his approach was one of the best ever . . ." (Graziella Sciutti)

There were about thirty orchestral rehearsals, with a constant turnover in orchestral personnel, until Cantelli felt satisfied that the musicians engaged were fully conversant with the Mozartian style he required. Once this was done, the orchestra had to be balanced with the singers on stage and this caused no end of problems, compounded by their working in a new theatre whose acoustical properties they had yet to master. Cantelli experimented with different orchestral layouts and the pit was elevated to narrow the gap between it and the stage. To assess the balance, Guido would hand over the baton to leader Enrico Minetti and listen from a midway position in the auditorium, yelling a pointed reprimand if any singer was below pitch.

Cantelli expected his singers to attend every rehearsal even if they were not singing. Occasionally this was not possible, due to prior committments. On one occasion, when Rolando Panerai failed to appear, he tartly observed, "A duet is impossible to be done with only one person." Fortunately Panerai's understudy was present, although he came forward admitting to Cantelli that he had not fully prepared the part. "Well take the score with you," responded Cantelli, "take the score with you, in order that we can continue the work." After a few bars Cantelli halted, accusing the understudy of simply "reading" the score. To which he replied that he was, "more or less." This was a reaction guaranteed to annoy Cantelli who screamed back, "More or less! You have to do what is written there, not more or less." Seething with rage, he walked over to the left-hand proscenium arch support, and, not thinking that behind its beautiful velvet covering lay bare wall, buried his fist deep into the pile, leaving a mark that may well still be visible today.

Not one detail of the production escaped Cantelli's attention. Sets, costumes, wigs — while dressing the ladies' hairstyles Guido would say: "We make a perfumed performance!" It's a fair bet too, that he had Despina bring real hot chocolate to Fiordiligi and Dorabella in the first act, but Graziella was a little vague on that point. After the final dress rehearsal, Cantelli invited the cast to dinner at Biffi Scala (the restaurant set into one corner of the Scala building). Still unable to relax Guido told them, like a football manager lecturing his team before an important match, that after their meal they should go home and have an early night: which by all accounts they did!

For the Milanese public, brought up on a diet of Verdi and Puccini, the sheer beauty of Mozart's music came as quite a shock. *Così fan tutte* became a sensational success, with demand for tickets running far in excess of the capacity of the 600-seat theatre. A further two performances were added to the original six, and as the run proceeded, it was announced that new contracts were being drawn up for an expected twenty performances during the 1956/57 season. La Scala had also received invitations to appear at the Johannesburg Festival later in the year and at Edinburgh in 1957, with *Così fan tutte* among the operas requested.

The success of the production in no way brought about a relaxation in Cantelli's demands, if anything they became even more rigorous. "During the bowing, he came up to us and immediately commented on whatever had happened during the performance. It always happens, the perfection that we strive for but is so difficult to attain. 'So you came a bit of a second late, you stopped a little too long there,' or, 'you came too fast,' or, 'that recitative was a bit muddled up.' While we were bowing and smiling, each one of us got a note — 'Tomorrow at ten o'clock, there will be a rehearsal.'" (Graziella Sciutti)

"The production was wonderfully organised, it was a very wonderful interpretation. The musical idea of Mozart by Guido is sublime, it seemed as if all his life he had played Mozart. In this performance of Mozart, he was between the German and Italian traditions. Italian people sometimes change Mozart's wit — [aping] Rossini — but the Germans don't always appreciate that Mozart wrote *Così fan tutte*, *Nozze di Figaro* and *Don Giovanni* in the Italian language, because Mozart needed the Italian language to be near the Italian style. This is the reason *Così fan tutte* from Cantelli, was a mixture of Italian and German style and his interpretation was exactly right." (Franco Mannino)

Dr. Ghiringhelli described Cantelli's production as: "One of the most perfect performances I ever heard."

Something like six months elapsed before the cast of *Così fan tutte* reassembled, towards the end of a very warm August, to prepare for Johannesburg. In these performances, Jacqueline Brumaire assumed the role of Fiordiligi, the rest of the cast being unchanged. An air of apprehension hung over everyone, as they feared that, after such a long break, Cantelli would begin rehearsing as though starting from scratch. Their fears proved groundless with contentious details being dealt with very quickly and Cantelli was soon able to call for a final run-through, held late one night in the main auditorium.

Luigi Alva, Panerai and Calabrese arrived straight from a meal at Biffi Scala, all three determined not to over-tax their voices. "At nine o'clock the orchestra was still warming up, and Guido started to come on stage wearing his grey shirt [the famous conducting jacket]. Nobody noticed him at that moment, he didn't say anything, just folded his arms, and in ten seconds the whole orchestra was in absolute silence. Then he opened his arms and started the overture, and from that moment it was a pity that rehearsal was not recorded. After the perfection of that overture, the first who has to sing is me — and I'm not going to sing! I open my mouth and start to sing like at a performance, and believe me, it was a fantastic rehearsal. Everyone was singing in full voice, just through the atmosphere he created." (Luigi Alva)

The whole work was played through without a pause and when Guido put down his baton he was smiling. "You see," he said, "this is the result of the way we have been working last season. This is what happens." Cantelli had praised his fellow musicians, something he rarely did.

*

A massive operation was involved in transporting the Scala company to

Johannesburg, and this was the first time in their history that they had performed outside Europe. Everyone, from stage hands to management, seemed to be crammed into one of the three planes ferrying them to South Africa, a journey of twenty-six hours and three refuelling stops. Indeed all that appeared to be left in Milan was the Scala Theatre itself.

The first Johannesburg Festival was being mounted by the city to celebrate the Seventieth anniversary of its foundation. In planning the ambitious programme, the organisers had looked to Edinburgh and Salzburg as models of the type of festival they envisaged. The festival included a drama season, featuring plays by local writers (including a couple in Afrikaans), works by George Bernard Shaw, in celebration of his centenary and a production of Terence Rattigan's "The Sleeping Prince" with Moira Lister. However, the core of the festival was its musical events. Claudio Arrau and Yehudi Menuhin performed concerts with the South African Broadcasting Corporation Symphony Orchestra and the London Symphony Orchestra gave five concerts. These were to have been conducted by Josef Krips, but he became indisposed at the last minute and with only a week's notice Jascha Horenstein took over all his programmes — no easy feat as they included, Mahler's *Resurrection* Symphony, Mozart's Fortieth and *Jupiter* Symphonies, the Beethoven *Eroica*, Walton's First Symphony and a Brahms programme. There were recitals by Segovia, concerts by I Musici and Margot Fonteyn and Michael Somes joined leading South African dancers. South Africa's own singing star Mimi Coertse gave a collection of popular arias.

La Scala took three productions to the festival, Donizetti's *L'elisir d'amore*, produced by Franco Enriquez and conducted by Antonino Votto; the Strehler/Sanzogno, *Il matrimonio segreto* and *Così fan tutte*. All their performances were given at His Majesty's Theatre on Commissioner Street in the city centre. Two previous theatres had stood there, with the present one being erected in 1946. With 1200 seats, it had double the capacity of Piccola Scala and the pit, normally occupied by show bands, allowed the forty or fifty musicians plenty of room. No production changes were necessary and once the curtains parted, the singers found they were able to recreate the exact feeling of performing at La Scala. The season opened with *L'elisir d'amore* on September 22, with *Così fan tutte* receiving its first performance two days later. (That same night Mantovani was in concert at the Plaza Theatre, whilst on the 25th Sir Malcolm Sargent conducted the SABC Symphony in the world *première* of Walton's *Johannesburg Festival Overture*.)

Cantelli directed eight performances of *Così fan tutte* and also found time to lead the Piccola Scala Orchestra in two concerts — their only orchestral appearances. After the first concert, given in the University Great Hall, Oliver Walker headlined his review in the "Johannesburg Star", "Cantelli has the grace of a bull-fighter." He then went on to elucidate:

GUIDO CANTELLI is a conductor who always appears to be in silhouette. Seen thus his trim, slim, faultlessly tailored figure has the shadowy grace of a Paganini cut-out. But once in motion quite another image suggests itself.

I thought then ... of a matador, a Belmonte spreading his arms and shoulders upward like wings to execute a veronica that could whirl the onrushing orchestral sound around him like a cloak yet leave him cool, poised and inviolate at the very heart of the tempest.

Cantelli is alone among younger conductors today for such poetry of gesture. I am not so foolish as to suggest that the art of conducting is the art of gesture. But it is a good two-thirds of it and when, for its answer, the gesture gets a musical response to match it in shapeliness and style, then it seems futile to argue over cause and effect.

After 20 years Furtwängler could say that he never thought of the role of the left hand in conducting. Cantelli's left hand shows what it can be. For its own good purposes it is as eloquent as Pierre Fournier's [another festival soloist] climbing the heights of his A-string.

Oliver Walker then analyses Cantelli's interpretations:

... I felt a special tenderness reserved for Wagner's *Siegfried Idyll*, that long essay on the pleasures of twilight sleep which can be more deadly to critics than the drops that Puck administered to Titania. Freshness, buoyancy and a spirit of luminous expectancy were instilled under Cantelli's pleading hands ...

We found him too urgent in the second movement of Haydn's Symphony No. 93. Here in this pastoral backwater we felt an urge to linger with Amaryllis in the shade. But Cantelli would have none of it and pressed on relentlessly to the hay-making jollity of the finale...

Rossini's *L'Italiana in Algeri* [Overture] and Mendelssohn's *Italian* Symphony sparkled with Mediterranean virtues which if allowed too much licence, can become barrel-organ. Cantelli alternately drove and rode them with spur and whispered confidence till they swaggered like veterans in new uniforms.

Despite many calls Cantelli refused to concede an encore to the packed hall. His manner once again suggested that of a bull-fighter who had achieved his moment of artistic truth and for that there could be no postscript.

Cantelli's second concert was given in City Hall, and prompted a banner headline in the Rand Daily Mail: "HUNDREDS COULDN'T GET IN AT CANTELLI CONCERT AND AUDIENCE WOULDN'T LET HIM GO." As the initialed reviewer D.L.S. explained:

HUNDREDS were turned away from the Cantelli farewell concert last night ... When the hall opened a long queue was waiting for possible returns, but the box-office manager explained that all seats had been sold by Friday night.

Even after the concert had begun there were still some people waiting in vain hope.

Enthusiasm ran so high that even La Scala orchestra members were applauded on entry, and not only the leader (Enrico Minetti).

As for Cantelli, he had the house with him throughout, and the end of the concert was as eventful as the beginning. The audience stamped and shouted and refused to leave.

"Cantelli showmanship was brilliant in Piccola Scala concert," wrote Oliver Walker, who then described the scene at its close:

GUIDO CANTELLI showed brilliant showmanship in the way he presented two encores with Piccola Scala Orchestra ... The applause at the end from an audience of more than 2,000 was as loud and peremptory as a summer thunderstorm.

Cantelli answered it by coming back several times without his baton. In the end, when stamping feet joined the handclaps and shouts he tripped off with his hand outstretched towards the wings, where some unseen minion was guarding the magic wand.

His first encore, Rossini's *The Silken Ladder* overture, might have been written to show off his own clear graces as a conductor, and the Mediterranean sparkle which his small orchestra can mirror so luminously between the fiddles, wind sections and even the double-basses.

But the real master touch came with the second encore, the finale of Mendelssohn's *Italian* Symphony, which is marked *Saltarello*. The first "Saltarello" was actually Cantelli's as he bounded on to the dais and in mid-air, as it seemed, summoned up those four smashing chords which signal an orchestral scamper fast enough to lift conductor and audience on to tip-toe.

Churchill, when once congratulated on a witty aside in the House of Commons, admitted that some of his best extempores took a fortnight to prepare.

This last encore of Cantelli must have taken quite a time to rehearse, unless — as one or two neighbours seemed to imagine — it was just an accident that the whole band happened to have the parts of Mendelssohn's *Italian* Symphony on their stands at that moment.

The programme had included performances of the Beethoven and Prokofiev First Symphonies, with the Prokofiev being a Cantelli *première* — although it's doubtful if the critics were aware of that. About his performance, Oliver Walker wrote:

Cantelli's reading ... was intentionally wry, and so far as the Minuetto section went, a huge mockery, for the accents were grossly underlined as if the music had been designed as a ballet for pachyderms.

For D.L.S.:

... Cantelli in his wizardry made not an essay in pastiche but a brilliant piece of mimicry. How right that was! And the Gavotte was unmistakeably Russian in humour — impish Prokofiev and cunning Cantelli!

As to the Beethoven, for Oliver Walker, "Pastoral happiness shone through the performance . . ." The first violins had plucked the opening C raggedly but this did not mar the performance, as Mr. Walker continued:

Here and there sounded undertones of grandeur, but much of it might have been marked "Cantare" for that was its spirit, and beautifully did the fiddles lift their voices in unison.

D.L.S. heard in Cantelli's Beethoven premonitions of things to come:

He showed the No. 1 not as late Beethoven but nevertheless as great Beethoven. That dark introduction had intimations of the power to come.

The Minuet-Scherzo was a perfect pattern, perfectly modelled. In the final Allegro, light to the point of dazzlement, there was strong sinew under the incredibly agile movement. This was a great performance.

Despite the audiences' demonstrations of enthusiasm for Guido and his conducting, he felt very lonely after the performances. Iris and baby Leonardo were at home in Milan, and whenever they came in to his mind he was overcome by homesickness. Guido never allowed these feelings to come between himself and the music, but after giving of his artistic soul in performance, there was a void which only his family could fill. It was obvious to the members of the company how he felt and, in time, the company became another family to him. Guido found himself gravitating towards the three ladies in the cast, with whom he felt at ease and together they would let the tensions of a performance slip away over a meal.

Apart from these intimate evenings, the Scala company were invited to any number of official receptions and private parties organised by their South African hosts. With Guido Cantelli in their midst, few could resist the temptation to play one of his recordings. Whenever this happened, it was always noticeable that Guido concentrated intently on the music. He gave an impression of enjoying what he heard, while at the same time being alive to any shortcomings in the performance. One of these parties turned into a pretty noisy affair, with far too many people crammed into too little space. Blasting from the gramophone came the latest musical import from America — "Rock and Roll." Not surprisingly Guido retreated to a corner, where Graziella Sciutti found him and begged a dance. "I can't dance to that," he told her, "but if there's a waltz, I can do that." A Despina-ish twinkle in her eyes Graziella vanished into the crowd, returning to Guido's side, as the strains of a waltz replaced the insistent beat of Rock-and-Roll. Guido was no Fred Astaire, but as Graziella discovered, he could waltz — and well at that!

Everyone in the company regretted that a vast potential audience was excluded from their performances — almost certainly the only ones they would give in South Africa for the forseeable future — because the South African government did not relax their apartheid policy. As a spontaneous gesture, each morning groups of singers and musicians, Cantelli included, went into the areas where the black and coloured populations lived and put on a performance. They played in church halls, community centres and schools. Always they were greeted with enthusiasm; here there were no political barriers, just people brought together in a common love of music. The informal conditions led to much audience participation with singers and musicians answering questions and signing autographs. In return, a special concert was organised for the Scala company in which musicians from the different cultures each gave a recital of their own native music.

La Scala's performances at the Johannesburg Festival were a triumph beyond their wildest dreams and the common experience brought the company together and created that spirit of true ensemble which is the hallmark of the greatest opera companies. At a farewell reception given by La Scala, Cantelli was quoted in the "Johannesburg Star" as saying: "Our spirit, our soul — yes, our soul, has been very touched by the reception you have given us . . . Long life to Johannesburg, and long life to the Johannesburg Festival."

Spirits were high on the flight back to Milan, with an air of end-of-term celebration; at one stage a pillow fight was in progress! Guido sat next to Graziella, who remembered a strange conversation. As the plane hit a patch of turbulence she caught hold of Guido's arm to steady herself. Guido took it all calmly and with the air of someone who has seen it all before, assured her that it was all right. Pointing to the life line on his palm, he said, "See, it is long, with me you are safe."

*

Dr. Ghiringhelli had informed Cantelli during the first run of *Così fan tutte* that it was the unanimous decision of La Scala's management, that he was to be offered the position of Musical Director of Teatro alla Scala. Cantelli knew that by accepting the post he became the heir to a unique tradition at La Scala, that carried an unbroken line back to Verdi, forward through Toscanini and de Sabata. (It is, by the way, Dr. Ghiringhelli's opinion that the line ended with Cantelli.) There was no doubt about Guido Cantelli's musical abilities and he was fully aware of the responsibilities now placed upon him; but, at thirty-six, he had little or no experience of the myriad, non-musical aspects in the day-to-day running of the opera house that his position as musical director would bring him into contact with. Meanwhile plans were being made for future operatic productions under his direction. Graziella Sciutti, Rolando Panerai and Luigi Alva were already contracted for a production of *Don Pasquale*, and Guido was also to conduct *La sonnambula* with Maria Callas as Amina. (La Scala brought this production to Edinburgh in 1957, with Antonino Votto conducting.) He had not, however, yet conducted a really large-scale opera at La Scala, and to this end, was studying the possibilities of opening the 1957 season with *Otello*.

On October 25, Cantelli directed a Beethoven concerto programme at La Scala with Artur Rubinstein as soloist. A concert of Haydn, Ghedini, Strauss and Ravel followed on November 1. On November 16, La Scala made the official announcement of Guido's appointment as Musical Director and, to celebrate, he conducted the Scala Orchestra on the following day at Teatro Coccia. In fact, this was a double celebration — planned by both sides to coincide — as it marked the re-opening of the Coccia after a two-year closure for a complete restoration. A huge crystal chandelier made by Murano of Venice, at a reputed cost of four million lire (around £2,285 by 1978 rates of exchange) now adorned the ceiling, and under its dazzling light the freshly gilded auditorium, glowed with expectancy. At Cantelli's request, the theatre was lavishly decorated with flowers, with alternate boxes carrying bunches of roses, while evergreens and a profusion of blooms were draped over the orchestra pit, empty on this occasion as the orchestra was on stage. Guido had chosen four works for his celebratory programme: Rossini's *Semiramide* overture, Brahms's First Symphony, Strauss's *Don Juan* and Ravel's *La valse*.

"Cantelli you're phenomenal," a voice cried out from the gallery after one work, and this was joined by others calling: "Bravo," and "Viva Cantelli," as though history were repeating itself. From the moment Guido had stepped on to the stage, his audience had risen as one man to applaud him and each work was received with torrents of acclamation. Overwhelmed by this reception, Cantelli conducted as though in a trance, pouring his heart and soul into every note. Only during the interval did he come back to reality as he embraced the Maestro Felice Fasola, in a brief and touching reunion.

A continuous crescendo of applause greeted the performance of *La valse*. As a young student in Rome, Graziella Sciutti remembered hearing Cantelli direct this work (in all probability the same performance referred to by Franco Ferrara) and to this day she can recall its effect, which is worth noting in this context: "If it is not done to perfection, it can be extremely uninteresting . . . suddenly for the first time I felt with this piece, to be surrounded by the music, and this music came from the body of this man. It was not only the orchestra playing it, but there was a unity from the movement, from the charisma that came out of Cantelli and swept through the theatre." When Graziella talks of how the music, "came from the body of this man," it's a description of Cantelli remarkably

Reproduced by courtesy of Signor De Angelis, Secretary, Teatro Coccia.

close to one given by Folco Perrino. He remembered attending a concert given in Turin by Cantelli and the Scala Orchestra. In order to observe Cantelli at close quarters, Perrino sat in the second row. As Cantelli conducted Folco Perrino says he witnessed quite distinctly a kinetic force emanating from Cantelli's body, and that he appeared to be surrounded by a white halo. Perrino's only explanation for this extraordinary manifestation was that, due to Cantelli's high energy output, his body was generating an inordinate amount of static electricity.

The audience at Teatro Coccia was determined not to let Cantelli go and he was recalled time and time again to the front of the stage. Finally he gave the audience what they wanted — not one, but two encores. The first was by Verdi, the second — Handel's *Largo* — was the last piece of music Guido Cantelli ever conducted.

A reception for Cantelli, the orchestra and officials of La Scala, was held at the Unione Club (which occupies a small suite at Teatro Coccia) and Cantelli publicly thanked his orchestra, saying that they had surpassed even what he thought of as their best: "This evening, here in my own town, I feel embarrassed, and I want to view a final great gift. I want to view your heart, because in your most passionate performance, Novara seemed to me to be yours."

Privately, Guido told Piero Olivieri — whose father had sold him his first scores and records — that he had three reasons why he was so happy at this moment: his success in his home town, his appointment at La Scala and his love for his son.

On the day following this evening of enchantment the name "Cantelli" was on everyone's lips: but the familiar figure himself was standing on his "spot" at Novara Stadium, having dashed there from Milan in order to be in time for the kick-off. Guido was asked why he did not go to New York, for his forthcoming season, by boat, thus giving him time for a few days rest. "Impossible," he replied, "because on Monday the twenty-sixth, I have to have the baton in my hand in New York." As Guido bade farewell to his fellow supporters, he hoped that his beloved Novara team would keep up their form until he returned in January.

*

Legend would like us to believe that Guido Cantelli boarded his plane to New York knowing that he would never complete the journey. The Philharmonic Symphony concerts were taking him away from his work at La Scala, and he was not looking forward to them, as they were little more than a contractual obligation that had to be fulfilled.

All manner of emotional and prophetic scenes are supposed to have been played out, as Guido said goodbye to Iris for the last time. As Iris Cantelli recalled, Guido said nothing in particular as they waited in the departure lounge of Rome's Ciampino Airport. Only as he left to board the aircraft, did Guido become excited, because at that moment film stars Ava Gardner and Walter Chiari were arriving, and Guido wanted to catch a glimpse of them, particularly Miss Gardner. Leaving Iris, he said, "I'm sorry to leave you, I will see you soon, but I go there to see Ava Gardner." And he was gone. Their original plans were for Iris to join Guido in New York after a week or ten days, with Leonardo remaining in Milan, under the care of a nurse. (While I was researching this biography, many people asked me to find out what became of Cantelli's son. Leonardo lives with his mother in Rome, and has all the usual interests of a person his age. When I met him in May 1978, Leonardo was pursuing an academic career.) When Iris returned to Via Livorno, she found a collection of letters that Guido had written, and hidden around their apartment. In one he asked Iris, "Please paint again, because you are only a good painter."

The flight to New York held in prospect a very gruelling journey with scheduled stops at Milan, Paris, Shannon and then the long hop across the Atlantic. Visibility was poor as the DC6-B of Linee Aeree Italiane (now part of Alitalia) left Rome at 6.40 GMT. Nothing indicated that this flight would be any different from the hundreds of others the airline regularly flew. The particular plane Cantelli was aboard had only been in service a few weeks and the DC6-B — a large plane — had an excellent safety record. Fog prevented a landing at Milan, so the pilot Captain Attilio Vazzoler — very experienced on the transatlantic run — headed straight for Paris. By the time refuelling and pre-flight checks were completed, thirty-five people had boarded (some reports say thirty-four). With ten crew and the two passengers who boarded at Paris, the passenger list included fourteen Americans and one Turk, the rest being Italian.

Light snow — the first winter snowfall over Paris — caressed the wings and body of the DC6-B as it taxied along Orly's runway at midnight, seconds into Saturday November 24. Take off appeared to be normal, but then the plane seemed to have trouble gaining altitude. Two miles out from Orly, over the village of Paray-Vieille-Poste, according to eyewitnesses one or more of the engines broke away from the fuselage. An engine certainly fell to the ground, imbedding itself deep into the outside wall of a house. Flames were coming from the plane as it descended, hitting a two-storey house in the village and completely destroying it, killing a small boy and injuring two of the occupants. Fully-loaded with fuel, the plane fell to ground behind Paray-Vielle-Poste's town hall and a massive explosion occurred on impact sending up a pillar of flame that could be seen in Paris.

Within minutes, scores of fire engines and police vans were on the scene. There was very little they could do, the intense heat and flames made it practically impossible to get anywhere near the wreckage, which hardly even resembled an aeroplane. Twenty-five bodies were taken from the site to Paray's city hall, where local residents kept a candlelight vigil as the crash had severed all electricity supplies. Reports speak of two survivors, Nicodeme Finamore and his wife Concetta (Consolina, in an

Italian report). They were on their way to Shannon, where Nicodeme was the airline's chief engineer. Both were taken to hospital, where Concetta had a leg amputated. Extensive research at Alitalia's archive in Rome has failed to locate the Finamores, but it is possible that Nicodeme died some years later, on account of the severe burns he received.

Cantelli's body was virtually cremated in the inferno and legend says that he was recognised by the hand-made shoes he was wearing which had the name "Cantelli" stamped inside. Dr. Ghiringhelli told me that Cantelli's body was identified by his brightly-coloured pullover — a fragment of the material still intact under his arms being enough to establish positive identification.

As news of Cantelli's death came through, La Scala cancelled their next scheduled performance. At their Festival Hall concert on November 25 the Philharmonia, under Hans Swarowsky, dedicated a performance of Mozart's Overture to *Die Zauberflöte* to Cantelli's memory.

Cantelli had split his eight-week New York season in two and it was here that his absence from the podium would first be brought home. He was to have given four weeks from November 29 and return for the remainder commencing March 14, 1957. The opening programmes were to have featured the first American performance of Ghedini's Concerto for Orchestra but the score and parts were destroyed along with their conductor. Dmitri Mitropoulos took over these concerts giving an entirely different programme, which he dedicated to Cantelli, and which included Prokofiev's Fifth Symphony. All Cantelli's remaining concerts were given as originally planned and conducted by Leonard Bernstein and Paul Paray.

Memorial services were held in London and New York: in New York on November 30 a Requiem Mass for Cantelli was celebrated at St. Malachy's Roman Catholic Church, 239 West 49th Street. Msgr. James B. O'Reilly officiated, and John Corigliano, the concert master of the Philharmonic Symphony, played Handel's *Largo* with the organist of St. Malachy's, composer Paul Creston. In London, a Requiem was celebrated by Father J. Law at St. James's, Spanish Place on December 11. During the service Lois Marshall sang the *Pie Jesu* from Fauré's *Requiem*, and the choir sang the *Requiem* by Casciolini.

Almost a year after Cantelli had stepped off the podium at the Festival Hall for the last time, a public tribute to him was mounted. On June 23, the Philharmonia gave a performance of the Verdi *Requiem* conducted by Argeo Quadri. There is very little point in mentioning this performance, as nobody in the orchestra can recall anything about it, but the programme contained the most moving of all the written tributes paid to Cantelli, by Sir Beverley Baxter:

On an evening in June [*sic*] last year Guido Cantelli conducted Verdi's

Requiem here in the Festival Hall. It was a different Cantelli than we had known — more restrained, more thoughtful and more mature. No longer was he the eager youth who captured musical London in a single night shortly after the end of the war.

I met him first on that occasion and from time to time we renewed our friendship in the years that followed. Less than a year ago he came to my house after his concert and joined the family circle. Midnight struck its lament for the death of another day but he would not go home. When we ordered a taxicab an hour later he was like a small boy pleading to be allowed to stay up with his elders, almost as if he were afraid of the dark. It was the last time we saw him for he had a rendezvous with death.

It is hard to assess what would have been Cantelli's place in the Valhalla of the music gods if he had been allowed the fulfilment of the years. In his early period as a conductor he combined wistfulness and delicacy with a fiery uninhibited sense of the dramatic. When he conducted Mozart he might have been a professor of the ballet and when he conducted Tchaikovsky's Fifth he seemed to stretch to the towering stature of Boris Goudonov.

It is an ironic paradox that perhaps the one quality which Cantelli lacked as a conductor was sorrow. He had a sense of the heroic and a capacity for grief but it seemed to me that the gentleness and the beauty of sorrow had not yet come within his range. Perhaps it was because they had not come within his experience of life.

We cannot say what Guido Cantelli would have become with the maturing years. He will not grow old as we grow old. He lived in the springtime and the early summer of life and was never to know the dying autumn — tinted leaves and winter's sleep of death.

Cantelli's funeral took place on Saturday December 1. Early in the morning the coffin was privately transferred from the chapel of Milan's Monumentale Cemetery, where Cantelli's shattered body had lain on being returned from France. Members of the Scala Orchestra had taken turns to mount a guard of honour and for several days an uninterrupted stream of pilgrims came to pay their last respects. From the Monumentale the coffin was taken to the courtyard of Teatro alla Scala, next to the artist's entrance in Via Filodrammatici. Black decorations covered the walls and the coffin was placed in front of a large cross. Five crowns surrounded the cross, these had come from Teatro alla Scala, Orchestra del Teatro alla Scala, Dr. Ghiringhelli, Conservatorio di Musica "Giuseppe Verdi" Milano and Victor de Sabata. A sixth, made of red carnations carried a ribbon reading. "Il tuo Maestro — Arturo Toscanini." ("Your Maestro.") A wreath of red roses lay on the coffin, bearing the names of Iris and Leonardo.

At 10.30 the *cortège* moved into Piazza della Scala, pausing as the hearse reached the theatre's narrow front doors, open wide as if to admit a huge audience. Within could be seen the completely deserted stage and auditorium, bathed in the golden tints of the house lights. From the pit came the sound of Handel's *Largo* performed by a conductorless orchestra. This was the orchestra's personal tribute to Guido Cantelli. When they had asked permission to make this gesture de Sabata had offered to conduct but he was politely turned down. The musicians felt that with Cantelli so close to them he would be conducting them in one last performance.

Leaving Piazza della Scala, the *cortège* went through Corso Matteotti, across San Babila and into Via Monforte. Turning right into Via del Conservatorio — passing Gallini's as they did so — the *cortège* then made its way to the church of Santa Maria alla Passione. Along the route, vast crowds stood in silence, hardly believing that it was the funeral of Guido Cantelli passing before their eyes, remembering how many times over the years Guido had walked across the square in front of Santa Maria alla Passione on his way to the conservatory or Via Livorno. Now his remains were being taken inside his own parish church, and as they were borne across the threshold clergymen invited the crowd to, "Pray for the soul of Guido Cantelli." As the pall-bearers moved towards the high altar, the organist played Handel's *Largo*. The Provost, Giuseppe Sironi, conducted the service, during which the choir sang the *Requiem Aeternam* from the Verdi *Requiem*. At its conclusion, the coffin was returned to the hearse, and driven to Novara for burial.

A special dais had been constructed in the centre of the Basilica di San Gaudenzio to support the coffin and so great were the numbers wishing to attend the service that many spilled out into the area directly in front of the Basilica. Msgr. Gilla Vincenzo Gremigni, the Bishop of Novara, took the service. The choir, of which Cantelli had once been a member, sang the *Miserere* from the Verdi *Requiem*. During the service, Mayor Bermani of Novara said this of Cantelli: 'I would have given I don't know how many years of my life for him who was the best of us. But now all I can do is to bring him here within the boundaries of the town which was his."

All of Novara wanted to accompany Guido Cantelli on his last journey from the Basilica to the cemetery. A massive crowd followed behind the coffin, passing almost immediately the house where he was born. As they walked along the streets Cantelli knew so well, all the churches in Novara began a melancholy peeling of their bells which counterpointed the sound of Handel's *Largo* played by the town band. Music which only days before Guido had brought to life at the Coccia still appeared inspired by his direction.

Throughout, Cantelli had been accompanied by Dr. Ghiringhelli, Ghedini, representatives of Teatro San Carlo, La Fenice, Maggio Musicale Fiorentino and conductors Antonino Votto and Carlo Maria Giulini. Standing with them at the graveside were the entire Scala Orchestra, together with members of Cantelli's family; one old man stood alone with his thoughts — Maestro Felice Fasola. Only Iris did not attend, for her the events were so traumatic, that to be present would involve a strain far greater than she could bear.

All of them watched as the coffin of reddish wood was lowered into the vault containing the remains of other honoured men of Novara. Regaldi the poet, Tornielli the ambassador, Pasquali the senator, Coccia the composer and now Guido Cantelli — Conductor.

An ailing Toscanini was never told of Cantelli's death, the card bearing his name had probably been sent by the Toscanini family. It was reported in the "New York Times" that Toscanini was informed of Guido's death, as he was expecting him for dinner on the evening of November 25 but Toscanini's daughter Wally confirmed when I spoke to her that her father was definitely never told of Cantelli's death.

Arturo Toscanini died on January 16, 1957 — fifty-three days after Guido Cantelli.

*

Cantelli's death came at a watershed in his life; his artistic maturing was a continuous process but his acceptance of the post at La Scala was a change of direction. It would be possible to speculate where this might have taken him but it is better simply to remember Guido Cantelli as the thirty-six year-old conductor who died bequeathing a total artistic statement of himself.

There was nothing embryonic about Cantelli, he was from the start a great conductor, yet his career was really very short — just seven years on the international music scene from the time of his first NBC concerts — and this is undoubtedly the main cause of the eclipse of his reputation in recent years — compounded by the unavailability of most of his recordings. Had Cantelli's career lasted as long as Toscanini's he would still have been active around the year 2,000! Cantelli was meant for the latter half of the Twentieth century, in much the same way as Toscanini's career straddled the first half. Cantelli would have carried forward the positive artistic ideals of an earlier generation (of which Toscanini was part) because Cantelli was not a "modern" man. He was in a way, the last born of the generation that ended with the passing of Otto Klemperer and this in effect made him a man between generations. Far from producing a personality that was rootless, Cantelli's ever-questing mind enabled him to take from the past and the present, what he needed to build for himself an art that was as free as light, pure, authentic and luminous: but was to have such a short life. These last words apply equally to pianist Dinu Lipatti and violinist Ginette Neveu, as like Cantelli they would be struck down as their careers were bringing forth all they promised.

There is an added poignancy about this brief mention of their lives in a work on Cantelli, as a glance at their respective birthdates shows how close they were in time; Dinu Lipatti — 1917; Ginette Neveu — 1919; Guido Cantelli — 1920; seldom has there been an artistic deprivation of this magnitude.

Ultimately one comes to Cantelli's recorded legacy (and this refers to the commercial issues) preserved in a handful of performances. As one who only knows Cantelli through these, I have found, over the years that each time I return to them the musical experience renews itself with a new freshness and spontaneity, revealing some facet in the music seemingly not present at the last hearing. It is as though Cantelli were still here: still telling us what he had found in the music. The recordings show no trace of the agonies that went into their making for an inner serenity has somehow been caught by the microphones. There is a depth of sonority, tenderness and one is aware of an acute interpretative vision. Cantelli may be conducting, but it is the composer who comes across. Under this man's baton, the music seems to dance, continually in motion, with a marvellous forward pulse that is never overdriven. Here was a gift that eluded even Toscanini who could sometimes (although not as often as his detractors claim) be rigid and unbending, through Cantelli music flowed as pliable as a perfectly annealed piece of precious metal.

Each of Guido Cantelli's recordings preserves something unique. His Tchaikovsky Fifth captures the feeling of a Cantelli live performance (the 1952 NBC performance of this work, reveals how much deeper the interpretation had become over a period of two years, as this account can only be described as profound — the last word one would usually apply to this work). Curiously the Beethoven Seventh emerges as a rather muted work, especially when compared to Toscanini's incandescent recording of 1936 with the New York Philharmonic Symphony, but Cantelli's is the only version of this work you could actually dance to, in accordance with Wagner's description of it as the "apotheosis of the dance."

Miraculous is the only word I can use to describe the Debussy recordings, *Le martyre de St. Sebastien* ranking as one of the greatest orchestral recordings ever made and were the music not so feeble I would be inclined to nominate it as Cantelli's recorded masterpiece. To *La mer* he brought a Mediterranean warmth, diametrically opposed to Toscanini's interpretation which conjures up the icy whiplash fury of a storm-laden Atlantic. Above all, the sensuous poetry of *Prélude à l'après-midi d'un faune* is here truly a miracle, in whose final dying cadences Cantelli elicited from the Philharmonia a *diminuendo* that carries one to paradise.

Cantelli took more individual sessions over the Brahms Third Symphony, than any other work he recorded. For me the third movement, with its yearning melody on the cellos, epitomises more than anything else the very essence of Guido Cantelli's art. This can be argued over, his interpretations being subjected to penetrating analysis with the score and set against others. However, in the final reckoning, in discussing

Guido Cantelli, there is only one thing that matters — the theme which runs throughout this biography: the music! This is his everlasting legacy.

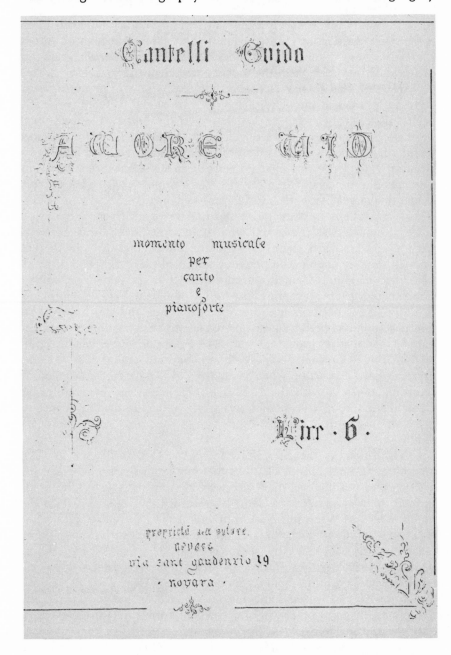

Title page, in Cantelli's own handwriting, of his unpublished song "Amore mio". Reproduced by courtesy of Mariangela Cantelli.

"AMORE MIO"
momento musicale per canto e pianoforte

Cosi fan tutte — Piccola Scala, January/February 1956. Above On stage, Act One (left to right) Rolando Panerai — Guglielmo, Franco Calabrese — Don Alfonso, and Luigi Alva — Ferrando. Below Cantelli assists Graziella Sciutti — Despina (centre) as they put the final touches to her mistress Fiordiligi's hair (Elisabeth Schwarzkopf — left), while a member of the production team looks on with approval (photos: Erio Piccagliani, Teatro alla Scala)

Royal Festival Hall. Above *Cantelli with Toscanini on stage during a rehearsal break for Maestro's Brahms cycle with the Philharmonia in Sept/Oct 1952. Between them is Herbert Downes (1945–74) the orchestra's principal viola, and to the extreme right Manoug Parikian (courtesy of London Express News and Features Services).* Below *In the conductor's room Cantelli talks enthusiastically to the Rt. Hon. Clement Attlee (there is no date recorded with this photograph to ascertain if Attlee was Prime Minister at the time) and his wife. Owen Mase looks on from the extreme right. The shadowy figure between Attlee and Cantelli is T.E. Bean, the Hall's general manager (photo: Paul Wilson)*

Royal Festival Hall. Above *With Cantelli in the conductor's room are (left to right) Renata Tebaldi, S.A. Gorlinsky, Francesco Molinari Pradelli, Martha Eggert, Jan Kiepura and Ferruccio Tagliavini.* Below *July 1956 — Cantelli directs two performances of the Verdi Requiem; with him are the soloists (left to right) Giuseppe Modesti, Ferruccio Tagliavini, Ebe Stignani and Elisabeth Schwarzkopf (photos: Paul Wilson)*

Via Livorno, 1956. Above *Cantelli in the living room with Iris, holds two beautiful replica stage-coaches which he found reposing in a junk shop during a London season (courtesy of Epoca Magazine, Milan).* Below *the Cantelli family: Iris, Leonardo and Guido (photo: Eugenio Coppini, Milan)*

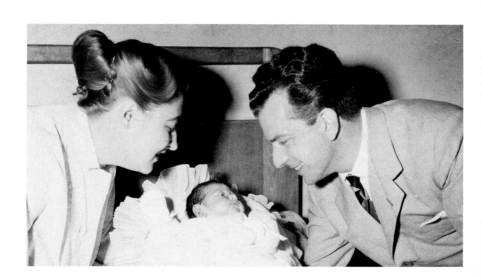

Above *Teatro Coccia,
November 17, 1956. Cantelli
leads the Scala Orchestra in
Handel's Largo, the final
encore and last work of
music he ever conducted.
This photograph must also
be counted the last ever
taken of him (courtesy of
Mariangela Cantelli).* Below
*The Cantelli memorial paid
for by public subscription in
the foyer of Teatro Coccia
(photo: Laurence Lewis)*

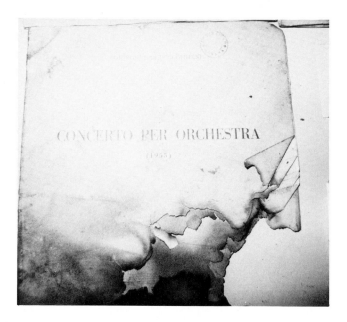

Above *A fragment of Ghedini's Concerto for Orchestra, salvaged from the wreckage of the plane in which Cantelli was killed. Ghedini kept this along with other fragments at Milan Conservatory, before handing them over to Novara Civic Museum where they were photographed. At the time they were not on public exhibition.* Below *The vault in which Cantelli's remains are buried and the tablet which records his name along with other honoured citizens of Novara (photo: Laurence Lewis)*

Above *Franco Mannino, in rehearsal at Monte Carlo, March 1977 (courtesy of Franco Mannino).* Below left *Franco Ferrara (courtesy of Franco Ferrara)* Below right *Novara, May 1978 — Cantelli is remembered by (left to right) Folco Perrino, Giuseppe Cantelli, Mariangela Cantelli, Angelo Bernasconi and Piero Olivieri (courtesy of Corriere di Novara)*

Guido Cantelli — a portrait dedicated to Georgina Mase (courtesy of Stuart and Jean Agrell)

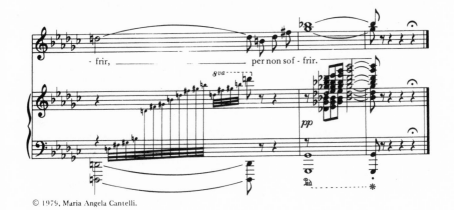

Amore mio, amore mio
spero talvolta dimenticarti
per non soffrire
ma quando poi t'avrò dimenticata
di che vivrò, perché vivrò.

Amore mio spero talvolta
dimenticarti per non soffrire
per non soffrire, per non soffrir
per non soffrir.

My love, my love
Sometimes I hope to forget you
So as not to suffer
But after forgetting you
What shall I live for, why shall I live.

My love, sometimes I hope
To forget you so as not to suffer
So as not to suffer, so as not to suffer
So as not to suffer.

NOTE:

On April 12, 1943, Guido Cantelli had published in Rome a collection of nine or ten songs. The scores of three survive and their number in the sequence is appended before each title.

2/ *Tornata E' Primavera.*
(Spring has just come.)

5/ *E' Un Valzer . . .*
(It's a Waltz . . .)

8/ *Margherita – a Tango.*

The texts are by Irma Merlo, a writer living in Novara, but are credited to Lorme, and Cantelli uses the pseudonym Oscar Cristalli.

APPENDIX 1

THE PERFORMANCES 1942–1949

Where details of programmes are known these are included.

1942

February 27. Milan — Conservatory.

April 20. Milan — Conservatory.

May 16. Milan — Conservatory.
During this concert, Cantelli directed a performance of his own *Theme with Variations*.

1943

February 21. Novara — Teatro Coccia.
Verdi La Traviata — with Gina Cigna (*Violetta*) and a cast including Giuseppe Manacchini, Laura Lauri, Alfredo Mattioli, Gino Lunardi, Giulio Zecca and Gino Foratesi.

1944

March 25, 26. Biella.
Puccini La Bohème.

April 10. Novara — Teatro Coccia.
Puccini Madama Butterfly — with Mirka Bereny (*Butterfly*), Mario Del Monaco (*Pinkerton*).

April 23. Novara — Teatro Coccia.
Massenet Werther — with a cast including Carla Lodetti, Emilio Ghirardini, Guido Uxa, Giuseppe Menni, and Maru Galliani (Falliani in another source).

April 29, 30. Novara — Teatro Coccia.
Concert with opera orchestra.

May 16, 18. Novara — Teatro Coccia.
Verdi La Traviata — with Margherita Carosio (*Violetta*) and a cast including Afro Poli, Giacinto Prandelli, Guido Uxa and Liana Avogadro.

November 12. Novara — Via Regaldi 2.
Chopin Polonaise, op.40/1, Ballad, op.47, Funeral March (from Sonata, op.35), Ballad op.23, Polonaise op.53/*Beethoven* Moonlight Sonata/*Weber* Invitation to the Dance/*Guido Cantelli* Intermezzo/*Liszt* Hungarian Rhapsody No. 2.
Cantelli's only formal piano recital was promoted by Gruppo d'Azione "Italia e civiltà" (Novara section) the cultural organisation of the occupying German forces. These were not present at the performance, but the programme carried a brief statement of German (Nazi) artistic ideals from Adolf Hitler.

1945

January 21, 22. Novara — Teatro Coccia. Concert.

January 25. Vercelli.
Puccini Tosca — with a cast including Jolanda Magnoni, Antonio Salvarezza, Giovanni Inghilleri and Guido Uxa.

February 17, 18. Vercelli.
Puccini Madama Butterfly.

March 14, 15. Vercelli.
Verdi Rigoletto.

July 27. Milan — Castello Sforzesco.
(See under *Orchestra del Teatro alla Scala*.)

August 19. Turin.
Broadcast concert for RAI, programme included *Tchaikovsky* Symphony No.
6.

October 13, 16. Modena.
Verdi La Traviata.

October 23. Milan — Teatro Olimpia.
Concert with chamber orchestra.

1946
February 11. Genoa — Palazzo Ducale.
Concert with chamber orchestra.

March 3. Milan — Casa Maino.

April 11. Turin.
Broadcast concert for RAI.

April 22. Milan — Casa Maino.

June 16. Milan — Casa Maino.

July 26. Turin.
Broadcast concert for RAI.

August 23. Rome — Basilica di Massenzio.
Orchestra del Accademia di Santa Cecilia.

September 22. Venice — Teatro La Fenice.
9th Festival Internazionale di Musica Contemporanea.
Orchestra del Teatro La Fenice: *Riccardo Nielsen* Musica per archi (1946),
Ildebrando Pizzetti Violin Concerto (1945) — with Michelangelo Abbado, the
composer conducting, *Frank Martin* Ballad for Flute, String Orchestra and
Piano (1945) — with Guido Novello, *Leonard Bernstein:* "Jeremiah" Sympony
(1943) with Ginerva Vivante, soprano.

October 13. Trieste.

November 24. Florence.
Maggio Musicale Fiorentino.

November 29, December 1. Venice — Teatro La Fenice.

December 27. Turin.
Broadcast concert for RAI — with Arturo Benedetti Michelangeli.

1947
January 3. Turin — Conservatorio Giuseppe Verdi.
Orchestra Sinfonica della RAI: *Rossini* Overture: Le siège de Corinthe, *Hindemith* Mathis der Maler, *Dvořák* Cello Concerto — with Benedetto Mazzacutai, *Ravel* La valse. (Broadcast by RAI.)

January 16. Bologna.

January 26. Florence.

February 24. Bologna.

March 12, 15. Milan — Teatro Nuovo.
Concert with chamber orchestra.

March 16. Brescia.
Concert with chamber orchestra, repeat of programme of March 12 and 15.

March 26. Rome.
Orchestra del Accademia di Santa Cecilia.

March 31. Cagliari.

April 10. Trieste.

April 22-29. Padova, Udine, Trieste, Venice.
Maggio Musicale Fiorentino. Florence Symphony Orchestra: *Verdi* Overture: I vespri siciliani, *Mendelssohn* Violin Concerto — with Abuzzi (?), *Beethoven* Symphony No. 8, *Ravel* La valse. (These were the concerts arranged for Allied troops stationed in Italy by Major Arthur Watson.)

October 26, 28. Naples — Teatro San Carlo.
Concert.

November 17. Genoa.

December 12. Turin — Conservatorio Giuseppe Verdi.
Orchestra Sinfonica della RAI: *Bartók* Concerto for Orchestra, *Roger-Ducasse*
Sarabande — with Chorus, *Ravel* Rhapsodie espagnole. (Broadcast by
RAI—their listing dates this concert December 14.)

1948
January 14, 18. Rome.
Orchestra del Accademia di Santa Cecilia.

February 20, 27. Bologna.

March 14. Genoa.

April 4, 9. Venice — Teatro La Fenice.

April 28. Vienna — Konzerthaus Gesellschaft, Grosser Konzerthaus Saal.
Vienna Symphony Orchestra: *Verdi* Overture: I vespri siciliani, *Tchaikovsky*
Piano Concerto No. 1 — with Franco Mannino, *Ravel* Rhapsodie espagnole,
Hindemith Mathis der Maler.

May 12. Naples — Teatro San Carlo.

May 21. Milan — Teatro alla Scala.
Orchestra del Teatro alla Scala: *Ravel* Rhapsodie espagnole, *Brahms* Violin
Concerto — with Nathian Milstein, *Busoni* Berceuse élégiaque, *Hindemith*
Mathis der Maler.

September 11, 12. Venice — Teatro La Fenice.
11th Festival Internazionale di Musica Contemporanea. Orchestra del Teatro
La Fenice:
Riccardo Nielsen L'incubo (The Nightmare) — with Piero Guelfi (*The Man*),
Luciana P. Bernardi (*The Woman*). Coro del Teatro La Fenice, director Sante
Zanon. Set by Max Huber. Film by Attilio Bazzini. First performance of a
monodrama by Elsa Pradella, based on a novel by Petrus Borel.
Milhaud Les malheurs d'Orphée — with Ottavio Marini (*Orphée*), Clara
Petrella (*Euridice*), Gino del Signore (*The Blacksmith/The Wild Pig*), Marcello

Cortis (*The Wagon-maker*), Silvio Maionica (*The Basket Seller/The Bear*), Luciana P. Bernardi (*The Fox/The Twin Sister*), Maria Bodurian (*The Wolf/The Older Sister*), Antonietta Astolfi (*The Younger Sister*) and Medy Fernstroem, Trudy Goth, Erna Gautheir, Mario Bini, Elio Dolfi (*Mimes and Ballerinas*). Produced by Aurel M. Milloss and choreographed by Medy Fernstroem. Sets by Enrico Paulucci. First performance in Italy of a three-act opera with libretto by Armand Lunel.

Menotti The Telephone — with Marisa Morel (Lucy), Silvio Maionica (Ben). Produced by Marisa Morel, set by Titina Rota. First performance in Italy of one-act *opera buffa*.

The following concert is out of sequence, but is listed here to retain the Venice Festival continuity.

September 19, 1954. Venice — Teatro La Fenice.
17th Festival Internazionale di Musica Contemporanea. Orchestra Sinfonica di Roma della Radiotelevisione Italiana: *Ghedini* Pezzo concertante, *Hindemith* Mathis der Maler, *Debussy* Le martyre de Saint-Sébastien, *Ravel*: Daphnis et Chloé: Suite No. 2.

September 22. Siena — L'Accademia Chigiana.
A concert devoted to music by Baldassare Galuppi (1706-1785).

September 23. Perugia — Sagra Musicale Umbra.
Cantelli began rehearsing but was dissatisfied and left.

October 30, 31, November 1. Brussels.

November 11, 14. Palermo — Teatro Massimo.
Concert.

1949
March 26, 31, April 1. Bologna.

November 4, 5, 6, 7, 8, 12, 13, 14. Brussels. There are no programme details for the Brussels dates in 1948 and 1949, but during them Cantelli directed performances of the Schumann Cello Concerto with Gregor Piatigorsky, and the Grieg Piano Concerto with Rudolf Firkušný.

ORCHESTRA del TEATRO ALLA SCALA

All performances given at Teatro alla Scala unless otherwise stated.

1945

July 27. Milan — Castello Sforzesco.
Weber Overture: The Ruler of the Spirits, *Tchaikovsky* Symphony No. 6, *Mangiagalli* Humoresque for Piano and Orchestra — with Marcello Abbado, *Sibelius* The Swan of Tuonela, *Rossini* Overture: Le siège de Corinthe.

1948

May 21.
Ravel Rhapsodie espagnole, *Brahms* Violin Concerto — with Nathan Milstein, *Busoni* Berceuse élégiaque, *Hindemith* Mathis der Maler.

1949

June 1.
Wagner A Faust Overture, *Franck* Symphony in D Minor, *Bartók* Concerto for Orchestra.

June 26. Novara — Teatro Coccia.

November 22. Bergamo — Teatro Donizetti.
November 31.
Bach Christmas Oratorio: Sinfonia to Part 2, *Haydn* Symphony No. 93, *Ghedini* Pezzo concertante — with Enrico Minetti, Mario Gorrieri (violins) and Tomaso Vladinoci (viola), *Ravel* La valse, *Tchaikovsky* Symphony No. 4.

1950

June 19, 20.
Monteverdi/Ghedini Magnificat, *Mozart* Requiem K.626 — with Renata Tebaldi, Maria Radev, Giacinto Prandelli, Cesare Siepi.

September 5. Edinburgh Festival — Usher Hall.
Schubert Symphony No. 2, *Ghedini* Concerto dell 'Albatro — with Ornella

Puliti Santoliquido (piano), Enrico Minetti (violin), Massimo Amphiteatroff (cello), Leslie French (narrator), *Tchaikovsky* Symphony No. 5.

September 6. Edinburgh Festival — Usher Hall.
Haydn Symphony No. 93, *Stravinsky* Chant du rossignol, *Rossini* Overture: Semiramide, *Beethoven* Symphony No. 7, *Verdi* Overture: I vespri siciliani. (The Haydn, Stravinsky and Rossini pieces were broadcast on the BBC Home Service).

September 8. Edinburgh Festival — Usher Hall. *Monteverdi/Ghedini* Magnificat, *Mozart* Requiem K.626 — with Renata Tebaldi, Fedora Barbieri, Giacinto Prandelli, Cesare Siepi. (Broadcast — BBC Third Programme.)

September 10. Edinburgh Festival — Usher Hall.
Monteverdi/Ghedini Magnificat, *Tchaikovsky* Symphony No. 5.

September 22. Royal Opera House, Covent Garden.
Mozart Requiem K.626 — with Suzanne Danco, Fedora Barbieri, Giacinto Prandelli, Cesare Siepi, *Beethoven* Symphony No. 7, *Verdi* Overture: I vespri siciliani.

September 25. Royal Albert Hall.
Monteverdi/Ghedini Magnificat, *Ghedini* Concerto dell'Albatro — with Ornella Puliti Santoliquido (piano), Enrico Minetti (violin), Massimo Amphiteatroff (cello), Leslie French (narrator), *Tchaikovsky* Symphony No. 5.

October 2, 4.
Monteverdi/Ghedini Magnificat, *Schubert* Symphony No. 2, *Ghedini* Concerto dell'Albatro — with Ornella Puliti Santoliquido (piano), Enrico Minetti (violin), Massimo Amphiteatroff (cello), Giorgio Strehler (narrator), *Tchaikovsky* Symphony No. 5.

October 7, 9.
Mozart Symphony No. 29, K.201, *Stravinsky* Chant du rossignol, *Rossini* Overture: Semiramide, *Beethoven* Symphony No. 7.

October 29. Modena — Teatro Municipale.
Wagner Overture: Rienzi, *Schubert* Symphony No. 2, *Rossini* Overture: Semiramide, *Beethoven* Symphony No. 7.

November 12. Biella — Teatro Sociale.
Rossini Overture: Semiramide, *Beethoven* Symphony No. 7, *Tchaikovsky* Symphony No. 5, *Verdi* Overture: I vespri siciliani.

November 19. Como — Teatro Sociale.
Wagner Overture: Rienzi, *Schubert* Symphony No. 2, *Rossini* Overture: Semiramide, *Beethoven* Symphony No. 7.

November 21. Turin — Teatro Carignano.
November 22. Verona — Teatro Nuovo.
November 23. Brescia — Teatro Grande.
Rossini Overture: Semiramide, *Beethoven* Symphony No. 7, *Tchaikovsky* Sym-
phony No. 5. (The Turin concert was broadcast by RAI.)

1951
June 22, 23.
Frescobaldi/Ghedini Four Pieces, *Mendelssohn* Symphony No. 4, *Schönberg*
Theme and Variations, *Wagner* Siegfried Idyll, *Verdi* Overture: La forza del
destino.

September 24, 25.
Mozart Divertimento, K.287, Strauss Tod und Verklärung, *Ghedini* Partita,
Ravel La valse.

1952
June 19, 20.
Cherubini Symphony in D, *Bartók* Music for Strings, Percussion and Celesta,
Tchaikovsky Symphony No. 6.

June 24, 25.
Vivaldi Le quattro stagioni, *Schubert* Symphony No. 8, *Britten* Sinfonia da
Requiem (First Milan performance), *Rossini* Overture: Guillaume Tell.

September 23.
Andrea Gabrieli/Ghedini La battaglia, *Stravinsky* Jeu de cartes, *Weber* Overture: Euryanthe, *Brahms* Symphony No. 1.

1953
June 12, 13.
Rossini Overture: Le siège de Corinthe, *Dvořák* Symphony No. 9, *Prokofiev*
Alexander Nevsky — with Oralia Dominguez (soprano), La Scala Chorus.

October 7, 9.
Rossini Overture: La Cenerentola, *Schubert* Symphony No. 9, *Casella* Paganiniana, *Debussy* La mer.

1954

June 24, 25.
Beethoven Overture:Egmont, Piano Concerto No. 4 — with Artur Rubinstein, Symphony No. 7.

November 10, 11.
Schumann Manfred Overture, *Marinuzzi* Fantasia quasi passacaglia, *Debussy* Nuages and Fêtes, *Ravel* Daphnis et Chloé: Suite No. 2.

November 12. Brescia — Teatro Grande.
Rossini Overture: L'italiana in Algeri, *Schumann* Symphony No. 4, *Debussy* Prélude à l'après-midi d'un faune, *Ravel* Daphnis et Chloé: Suite No. 2.

1955

June 13, 14.
Beethoven Overture: Coriolan, Piano Concerto No. 5 — with Wilhelm Backhaus, Symphony No. 5.

Between September 26 and October 6, 1955, Cantelli took the orchestra on an eight-city European tour, giving concerts on the following dates: September 26 — Nice, September 27 — Marseilles, October 1 — Antwerp, October 2 — Brussels, October 3 — Amsterdam — Concertgebouw, October 4 — Hamburg, October 5 — Dusseldorf, October 6 — Monaco.

Cantelli gave two programmes, but there are no details as to which he gave on each date: *Rossini* Overture: La gazza ladra, *Ghedini* Pezzo concertante, *Debussy* La mer, *Beethoven* Symphony No. 5; and *Vivaldi* Concerto Grosso in D minor, *Brahms* Symphony No. 1, *Casella* Paganiniana, *Ravel* Daphnis et Chloé; Suite No. 2.

October 17, Teatro Elena.
Rossini Overture: La gazza ladra, *Brahms* Symphony No. 1, *Beethoven* Symphony No. 5.

November 1.
Vivaldi Concerto Grosso in D minor. *Brahms* Symphony No. 1, *Beethoven* Symphony No. 5.

November 2, 3.
Vivaldi Concerto Grosso in D minor, *Brahms* Symphony No. 3, *Casella* Paganiniana, *Copland* El Salón México.

November 5. Bologna — Teatro Comunale.
Rossini Overture: La gazza ladra, *Ghedini* Pezzo concertante — with Enrico

Minetti and Mario Gorrieri (violins) and Tomaso Valdinoci (viola). (These artists took part in all subsequent performances), *Debussy* La Mer, *Beethoven* Symphony No. 5.

November 6. Trieste — Teatro Communale G. Verdi.
Vivaldi Concerto Grosso in D minor, *Brahms* Symphony No. 1, *Casella* Paganiniana, *Debussy* La mer.

November 7. Venice — Teatro La Fenice.
Vivaldi Concerto Grosso in D minor, *Casella* Paganiniana, *Ravel* Daphnis et Chloé: Suite No. 2, *Beethoven* Symphony No. 5.

November 9. Perugia — Teatro Morlacchi.
November 10. Rome — Teatro Argentina.
Rossini Overture: La gazza ladra, *Ghedini* Pezzo concertante, *Debussy* La mer, *Beethoven* Symphony No. 5.

November 12. Palermo — Teatro Massimo.
Rossini Overture: La gazza ladra, *Ghedini* Pezzo concertante, *Debussy* La mer, *Brahms* Symphony No. 1.

November 14. Catania — Teatro Massimo Vincenzo Bellini.
Vivaldi Concerto Grosso in D minor, *Beethoven* Symphony No. 5, *Casella* Paganiniana, *Ravel* Daphnis et Chloé: Suite No. 2.

November 16. Genoa — Teatro Comunale Dell'Opera.
Vivaldi Concerto Grosso in D minor, *Ghedini* Pezzo concertante, *Debussy* La mer, *Brahms* Symphony No. 1.

November 17. Alessandria — Teatro Virginia Marini.
Rossini Overture: La gazza ladra, *Ghedini* Pezzo concertante, *Ravel* Daphnis et Chloé: Suite No. 2, *Beethoven* Symphony No. 5.

1956

January 27, 29, 31, February 3, 9, 19, 22, 26. Piccola Scala.
Mozart Così fan tutte — with Elisabeth Schwarzkopf (*Fiordiligi*), Nan Merriman (*Dorabella*), Graziella Sciutti (*Despina*), Roland Panerai (*Guglielmo*), Luigi Alva (*Ferrando*), Franco Calabrese (*Don Alfonso*). (Mariella Angioletti took the place of Nan Merriman in the February 26 performance.) Chorus Master — Norberto Mola, Harpsichord Continuo — Elio Cantamessa. Sets by Nicola Benois. Design by Eugene Berman. Costumes by Arturo Brambilla. Produced by Guido Cantelli.

September 24, 27, 29, October 1, 4, 6, 10, 12. Johannesburg Festival — His Majesty's Theatre.
Mozart Così fan tutte.
(As performances at Piccola Scala, except that Jacqueline Brumaire took over from Schwarzkopf as Fiordiligi.)

October 7. Johannesburg Festival — University Great Hall.
Rossini Overture: L'Italiana in Algeri, *Haydn* Symphony No. 93, *Wagner* Siegfried Idyll, *Mendelssohn* Symphony No. 4.

October 14. Johannesburg Festival — City Hall.
Rossini Overture: Il Signor Bruschino, *Mozart* Ein musikalischer Spass, K.522, *Prokofiev* Symphony No. 1, *Beethoven* Symphony No. 1, *Mendelssohn* Symphony No. 4 — 4th Movement.

October 25, 26.
Beethoven Overture: Prometheus, Piano Concerto No. 3, Piano Concerto No. 5 — with Artur Rubinstein.

November 1, 2, 3.
Haydn Symphony No. 93, *Ghedini* Concerto for Orchestra, *Strauss* Don Juan, *Ravel* La valse.

November 17. Novara — Teatro Coccia.
Rossini Overture: Semiramide, *Brahms* Symphony No. 1, *Strauss* Don Juan, *Ravel* La valse, *Verdi* (work unidentified, probably an overture), *Handel* Largo.
Guido Cantelli's last concert.

NBC SYMPHONY ORCHESTRA

Prior to January 1951, all performances given in Studio 8H, thereafter Carnegie Hall.

1949

January 15.
Haydn Symphony No. 93, *Hindemith* Mathis der Maler.

January 22.
Ghedini Pezzo concertante, *Casella* Paganiniana, *Tchaikovsky* Overture: Romeo and Juliet.

January 29.
Wagner A Faust Overture, *Bartók* Concerto for Orchestra.

February 5.
Franck Symphony in D minor, *Ravel* La valse.

December 24.
Handel Overture: The Messiah, *Bach* Christmas Oratorio; Sinfonia to Part 2, *Tchaikovsky* Symphony No. 4.

December 31.
Haydn Symphony No. 94, *Stravinsky* Chant du Rossignol, *Wagner* Overture: Rienzi.

1950

January 7.
Mozart Symphony No. 29 K.201, *Hindemith* Mathis der Maler.

January 14.
Frescobaldi/Ghedini Four Pieces, *Beethoven* Symphony No.7.

December 4.
Mozart Ein musikalischer Spass, K.522, *Rossini* Overture: Semiramide, *William Schuman:* "Undertow" ballet.

December 11.
Milhaud Introduction and Funeral March, *Dallapiccola:* Marsia: suite, *Verdi* Overture: Il vespri siciliani, *Haydn* Symphony No. 93.

December 18.
Vivaldi Concerto Grosso No. 4 *Busoni* Tanzwalzer, *Beethoven* Symphony No. 5.

December 25.
Corelli Concerto Grosso No. 8, *Vivaldi* Winter — Le quattro stagioni, *Geminiani/Marinuzzi* Andante — Strings, Organ and Harp, *Monteverdi/Ghedini* Magnificat — with Ralph Hunter (organ) and the Robert Shaw Chorale.

1951

January 1.
Rossini Overture: Le siège de Corinthe, *Bartók* Concerto for Orchestra.

January 8.
Schubert Symphony No. 2, *Ghedini* Concerto dell'Albatro — with Mischa Mischakoff, (violin), Frank Miller (cello), Arthur Balsam (piano), Ben Grauer (narrator).

January 15.
Vivaldi Concerto in A minor for Two Violins — with Mischa Mischakoff and Max Hollander, *Geminiani* Concerto Grosso No.2, *Debussy* Le martyre de Saint-Sébastien, *Stravinsky:* Fireworks. (There is a discrepancy in this programme with one source listing the work by Geminiani and another the Tragic Overture by Brahms.)

January 22.
Mozart Symphony No. 29 K.201, *Don Gillis* Prairie Sunset — Portrait of a Frontier Town, *Musorgsky/Ravel* Pictures at an Exhibition.

December 1.
Mozart Overture: Le nozze di Figaro, *Mendelssohn* Symphony No. 4, *Ravel* Pavane pour une infante defunte, La valse.

December 8.
Geminiani/Marinuzzi Andante — Strings, Organ and Harp, *Vivaldi* Le quattro stagioni — with Mischa Mischakoff (Violin). Sonnets read by Ben Grauer.

December 15.
Brahms Symphony No. 3, *Roussel* Sinfonietta for strings, *Berlioz* Rákoczy March.

1952

February 2.
Vivald Concerto Grosso No. 4, *Tchaikovsky* Overture: Romeo and Juliet, *Ghedini* Pezzo concertante, *Verdi* Overture: La forza del destino.

February 9.
Wagner A Faust Overture, *Bartók* Concerto for Orchestra.

February 16.
G. Gabrieli Sacrae symphoniae; Canzona, *Monteverdi* Sonata sopra Sancta Maria — with Choir of twelve sopranos, *Franck* Symphony in D minor.

February 23.
Ghedini Partita, *Musorgsky/Ravel* Pictures at an Exhibition.

March 1.
Schulman A Laurentian Overture *Tchaikovsky* Symphony No. 5.

November 29.
Weber Overture: Euryanthe, *Paul Creston* Two Choric Dances, *Frank Miller* Procession (First performance), *Schumann* Symphony No. 4.

December 6.
Vivaldi Concerto in A flat for Two Violins — with Remo Bolognini and Daniel Guilet, *Brahms* Symphony No. 1.

December 13.
Mozart Symphony No. 29 K.201, *Bartók* Music for Strings, Percussion and Celesta.

December 20.
Haydn Symphony No. 88, *Stravinsky* Jeu de cartes, *Ravel* Bolero.

December 27.
Bach Christmas Oratorio: Sinfonia to Part 2, *Cherubini* Symphony in D, *Strauss* Tod und Verklärung.

1953

January 3.
Schubert Symphony No. 8, *Britten* Sinfonia da Requiem, *Wagner* Overture: Rienzi.

February 21.
Rossini Overture: Le siège de Corinthe, *Tchaikovsky* Symphony No. 6.

February 28.
Haydn Symphony No. 93, *Hindemith* Mathis der Maler. (This concert marked Cantelli's fifth anniversary with the orchestra, and duplicated his debut programme of January 15, 1949.)

December 20.
Barber Overture: School for Scandal, *Bruno Bettinelli* Due invenzioni, *Debussy* Le martyre de Saint-Sébastien, *Ravel* Daphnis et Chloé; Suite No. 2.

December 27.
Handel Largo, *Schubert* Symphony No. 9.

1954

January 3.
Frescobaldi/Ghedini Three Pieces, *Franck* Symphony in D minor.

January 10.
Beethoven Symphony No. 1, *Casella* Paganiniana, *Falla* Suite: El sombrero de tres picos.

January 31.
Haydn Symphony No. 88, *Hindemith* Concert Music for Brass and Strings, *Wagner* Overture: Rienzi.

February 7.
Andrea Gabrieli/Ghedini La battaglia, *Mozart* Divertimento K.287, *Ravel* La valse.

February 14.
Rossini Overture: La Cenerentola, *Tchaikovsky* Symphony No. 4.

February 21.
Stravinsky Chant du rossignol, *Beethoven* Symphony No. 5.

NEW YORK PHILHARMONIC SYMPHONY ORCHESTRA

All performances given in Carnegie Hall, unless otherwise stated.
Dates marked * indicate concert broadcast by CBS Radio network.

1952

January 3, 4, 6*.
Frescobaldi/Ghedini Four Pieces, *Monteverdi/Ghedini* Magnificat — with Westminster Choir, *Beethoven* Symphony No. 5.

January 17, 18.
Schulman A Laurentian Overture (First performance), *Menotti* Piano Concerto — with Rudolf Firkušný, *Schubert* Symphony No. 2, *Hindemith* Mathis der Maler.

January 19, 20*.
Schulman A Laurentian Overture, *Dvořák* Piano Concerto — with Rudolf Firkušný, *Schubert* Symphony No. 2 (omitted on 20th), *Hindemith* Mathis der Maler.

January 24, 25.
Rossini Overture: Semiramide, *Lalo* Symphonie espagnole — with Isaac Stern, *Busoni* Berceuse élégiaque, *Musorgsky/Ravel* Pictures at an Exhibition.

January 26, 27*.
Rossini Overture: Semiramide, *Liszt* Piano Concerto No. 1 — with Nicole Henriot-Schwitzer, *Busoni* Berceuse élégiaque, *Musorgsky/Ravel* Pictures at an Exhibition.

1953

March 5, 6.
Brahms Tragic Overture, *Bartók* Concerto for Orchestra, *Beethoven* Symphony No. 7.

March 8*.
Beethoven Symphony No. 7, *Bartók* Concerto for Orchestra, *Verdi* Overture: La forza del destino.

March 12, 13.
Mozart/Negrotti Symphony in C, *Beethoven* Piano Concerto No. 4 — with Claudio Arrau, *Debussy* Le martyre de Saint-Sébastien, *Ravel* Daphnis et Chloé. Suite No. 2.

March 14.
Mozart/Negrotti Symphony in C, *Paul Creston* Two Choric Dances, *Verdi* Overture: La forza del destino, *Debussy* Le martyre de Saint-Sébastien, *Ravel* Daphnis et Chloé; Suite No. 2.

March 15*.
Mozart/Negrotti Symphony in C, *Brahms* Tragic Overture, *Liszt* Piano Concerto No. 2 — with Claudio Arrau, *Debussy* Le martyre de Saint-Sébastien, *Ravel* Daphnis et Chloé: Suite No. 2.

March 19, 20, 22*.
Mozart Ein musikalischer Spass K.522, *Ghedini* Concerto dell'Albatro — with Leonid Hambro (piano), John Corigliano (violin), Laszlo Varga (cello), Adolf Anderson (narrator), *Wagner* A Faust Overture, Siegfried's Rhine Journey (Götterdämmerung), Overture: Rienzi (not broadcast).

March 25, 26.
Andrea Gabrieli/Ghedini La battaglia, *Mozart* Piano Concerto K.466 - with Rudolf Serkin, *Pizzetti* Preludio ad un altro giorno (first U.S. performance), *Musorgsky/Ravel* Pictures at an Exhibition.

March 28*.
Rossini Overture: Il Signor Bruschino, *Beethoven* Piano Concerto No. 1 — with Rudolf Serkin, *Musorgsky/Ravel* Pictures at an Exhibition.

1954

February 25, 26.
Gabrieli Canzon septimi toni à 8, *Bartók* Music for Strings, Percussion and Celesta, *Brahms* Symphony No. 1.

February 27.
Brahms Symphony No. 1, *Beethoven* Piano Concerto No. 5 — with Rudolf Serkin, *Rossini* Overture: La gazza ladra.

February 28*.
Gabrieli Canzon septimi toni à 8, *Bartók* Music for Strings, Percussion and

Celesta, *Beethoven* Piano Concerto No. 5 — with Rudolf Serkin, *Rossini* Overture: Semiramide.

March 4, 5.
Rossini Overture: La Cenerentola, *Dallapiccola* Marsia: suite, *Mendelssohn* Symphony No. 4, *Debussy* La mer.

March 6, 7*.
Dallapiccola Marsia: suite, *Mendelssohn* Symphony No. 4, *Debussy* La mer, *Rossini* Overture: L'italiana in Algeri (not broadcast).

March 11, 12, 14*.
Vivaldi Concerto Grosso in A, *Bach* Violin Concerto in A — with Jascha Heifetz (omitted on 14th), *Mozart* Divertimento K.287, *Mendelssohn* Violin Concerto — with Jascha Heifetz.

March 15.
Vivaldi Concerto Grosso in A, *Mozart* Divertimento K.287, *Rossini* Overture: La Cenerentola, *Mendelssohn* Symphony No. 4. (A private concert given at the Grand Ballroom, Plaza Hotel, New York for members and friends of the Philharmonic.)

March 18, 19, 21*.
Cherubini Symphony in D, *Strauss* Tod und Verklärung, *Busoni* Berceuse élégiaque, Tanzwalzer, *Ravel* Bolero.

1955
January 13, 14.
Bonporti Concerto Grosso in D, *Beethoven* Symphony No. 6, *Marinuzzi* Fantasia quasi passacaglia, *Musorgsky/Ravel* Pictures at an Exhibition, *Marcello/Bach* Adagio in D minor.

January 15.
Beethoven Overture: Egmont, Piano Concerto No. 5 — with Robert Casadesus, Symphony No. 6.

January 16*.
Mozart Overture: Le nozze di Figaro, *Beethoven* Piano Concerto No. 5 — with Robert Casadesus, *Musorgsky/Ravel* Pictures at an Exhibition.

January 20.
Barber Adagio for Strings, *Brahms* Symphony No. 3.
(The remainder of this concert, featuring works by Debussy, Respighi [Fontane

di Roma] and Ravel, was taken over by Franco Autori when Cantelli collapsed after directing the Brahms).

January 27, 28.
Mozart Symphony No. 29 K.201, *Dukas* L'apprenti sorcier, *Ghedini* Pezzo Concertante, *Tchaikovsky* Symphony No. 4.

January 29.
Paisiello: Overture: Nina, o sia la pazza per Amore, *Dukas* L'apprenti sorcier, *Haydn* Cello Concerto — with László Varga, *Tchaikovsky* Symphony No. 4. (There is a discrepancy in this programme. It is possible that at the last moment Cantelli substituted the Ghedini *Pezzo concertante*, in place of the overture by Paisiello.)

January 30*.
Mozart Symphony No. 29 K.201, *Dukas* L'apprenti sorcier, *Tchaikovsky* Symphony No. 4.

February 3, 4, 6*.
Verdi Requiem — with Herva Nelli, Claramae Turner, Richard Tucker, Jerome Hines, Westminster Choir.

March 3, 4.
Haydn Symphony No. 93, *Mozart* Piano Concerto K.467 — with Walter Gieseking, *Franck* Symphonic Variations — with Walter Gieseking, *Falla* Suite: El sombrero de tres picos.

March 6*.
Haydn Symphony No. 93, *Ravel* Pavane pour une infante défunte, *Mozart* Piano Concerto K.467 — with Walter Gieseking, *Falla* Suite: El sombrero de tres picos.

March 10, 11.
Vivaldi Spring and Summer from Le quattro stagioni — with John Corigliano, *Beethoven* Piano Concerto No. 3 — with Rudolf Serkin, *Piston* Toccata, *Copland* El Salón México.

March 13*.
Vivaldi Concerto Grosso in D, *Beethoven* Piano Concerto No. 3 — with Rudolf Serkin, *Piston* Toccata, *Copland:* El Salón México.

March 17, 18.
Rossini Overture: Le siège de Corinthe, *Brahms* Symphony No. 1, *Debussy* Nuages and Fêtes, *Ravel* Daphnis et Chloé: Suite No. 2.

March 19.
Rossini Overture: Le siège de Corinthe, *Barber* Adagio for Strings, *Brahms* Symphony No. 1, *Musorgsky/Ravel* Pictures at an Exhibition.

March 20*.
Rossini Overture: Le siège de Corinthe, *Brahms* Symphony No. 1, *Debussy* Nuages and Fêtes, *Ravel* Daphnis et Chloé: Suite No. 2.

March 24, 25.
Bach Air from Suite No. 3, *Beethoven* Symphony No. 7, *Vivaldi* Autumn and Winter from Le quattro stagioni — with John Corigliano. *Respighi* Pini di Roma.

March 27*.
Handel Largo *Beethoven* Symphony No. 7, *Barber* Adagio for Strings, *Respighi* Pini di Roma.

1955 U.S. nationwide tour.

April 20. Urbana — University of Illinois.
Vivaldi Concerto Grosso Op. 3 No. 11, *Brahms* Symphony No. 1, *Barber* Adagio for Strings, *Musorgsky/Ravel* Pictures at an Exhibition.

April 22. Kansas — Topeka.
Vivaldi Concerto Grosso Op. 3 No. 11, *Beethoven* Symphony No. 7, *Barber* Adagio for Strings, *Musorgsky/Ravel* Pictures at an Exhibition.

April 25. Texas — El Paso.
Rossini Overture: Le siège de Corinthe, *Brahms* Symphony No. 1, *Debussy* Nuages and Fêtes, *Ravel* Daphnis et Chloé; Suite No. 2.

April 26. Tuscon — University of Arizona.
Rossini Overture: Le siège de Corinthe, *Brahms* Symphony No. 1, *Barber* Adagio for Strings, *Copland* El Salón México.

April 29. Los Angeles — Shrine Auditorium.
Rossini Overture: Le siège de Corinthe, *Brahms* Symphony No. 1, *Barber* Adagio for Strings, *Musorgsky/Ravel* Pictures at an Exhibition.

April 30. California — San Diego.
Rossini Overture: Le siège de Corinthe, *Brahms:* Symphony No. 1, *Debussy* Nuages and Fêtes, *Ravel* Daphnis et Chloé: Suite No. 2.

May 5. San Francisco — Opera House.
Rossini Overture: Le siège de Corinthe, *Brahms* Symphony No. 1, *Debussy* Nuages and Fêtes, *Ravel* Daphnis et Chloé: Suite No. 2.

May 7. Oregon — Corvallis.
Rossini Overture: Le siège de Corinthe, *Beethoven* Symphony No. 7, *Barber* Adagio for Strings, *Musorgsky/Ravel* Pictures at an Exhibition.

May 8. Washington — Seattle.
Vivaldi Concerto Grosso Op. 3 No. 11, *Brahms* Symphony No. 1, *Debussy* Nuages and Fêtes, *Ravel* Daphnis et Chloé: Suite No. 2.

May 11. Utah — Salt Lake City.
Rossini Overture: Le siège de Corinthe, *Brahms* Symphony No. 1, *Debussy* Nuages and Fêtes, *Ravel* Daphnis and Chloé: Suite No. 2.

May 14. Colorado — Denver.
Vivaldi Concerto Grosso Op. 3 No. 11, *Brahms* Symphony No. 1, *Barber* Adagio for Strings, *Musorgsky/Ravel* Pictures at an Exhibition.

May 16. Iowa — Ames.
Rossini Overture: Le siège de Corinthe, *Brahms* Symphony No. 1, *Debussy* Nuages and Fêtes, *Ravel* Daphnis et Chloé: Suite No. 2.

May 18. Wisconsin — Madison.
Vivaldi Concerto Grosso Op. 3 No. 11, *Beethoven* Symphony No. 7, *Barber* Adagio for Strings, *Musorgsky/Ravel* Pictures at an Exhibition.

May 21. Chicago — Orchestra Hall.
Vivaldi Concerto Grosso Op. 3 No. 11, *Beethoven* Symphony No. 7, *Barber* Adagio for Strings, *Musorgsky/Ravel* Pictures at an Exhibition.

During September 1955 the orchestra undertook a European tour with Cantelli sharing the podium with Dimitri Mitropoulos. Full details of all Cantelli's programmes are not available, but those which are known can be found listed below. Cantelli opened the tour with a concert in Victoria Hall, Geneva — then went on to Paris, where critical response to him was somewhat muted. After Paris, the orchestra made its next appearance at the Edinburgh Festival.

September 6. Edinburgh Festival — Usher Hall.
Rossini Overture: Le siège de Corinthe, *Brahms* Symphony No. 1, *Debussy* Nuages and Fêtes, *Ravel* Daphnis et Chloé; Suite No. 2.

September 7. Edinburgh Festival — Usher Hall.
Barber Adagio for Strings, *Beethoven* Symphony No. 7, *Copland* El Salón
México, *Musorgsky/Ravel* Pictures at an Exhibition. (It was this programme
that originally billed a performance of Copland's Third Symphony.)

September 25. Milan — Teatro alla Scala.
Rossini Overture: Le siège de Corinthe, *Brahms* Symphony No. 1, *Barber*
Adagio for Strings, *Musorgsky/Ravel* Pictures at an Exhibition.

1956

March 15, 16, 18*.
Paul Creston Dance Overture, *Schumann* Symphony No. 4, *Beethoven* Piano
Concerto No. 4 — with Wilhelm Backhaus.

March 22, 23.
Britten Sinfonia da Requiem, *Strauss* Don Juan, *Beethoven* Piano Concerto
No. 5 — with Walter Gieseking.

March 24.
Vivaldi Concerto Grosso Op. 3 No. 11, *Schumann* Symphony No. 4, *Britten*
Sinfonia da Requiem, *Rossini* Overture: Semiramide.

March 25*.
Vivaldi Concerto Grosso Op. 3 No. 11, *Beethoven* Piano Concerto No. 5 —
with Walter Gieseking, *Strauss* Don Juan, *Rossini* Overture: Semiramide (not
broadcast).

March 29, 30, 31, April 1*.
Wagner Good Friday Music (Parsifal), *Verdi:* Te Deum (Quattro pezzi sacri)
— with Westminster Choir, *Brahms* Alto Rhapsody — with Martha Lipton,
Monteverdi/Ghedini Magnificat — with Westminster Choir.

April 5, 6.
Haydn Symphony No. 88, *Hindemith* Concert Music for Brass and Strings,
Brahms Piano Concerto No. 1 — with Rudolf Firkušný.

April 8*.
Handel Largo, *Brahms* Piano Concerto No. 1 — with Rudolf Firkušný,
Hindemith Concert Music for Brass and Strings, *Berlioz* Rakoczy March (not
broadcast).

154   *Guido Cantelli*

(The following programmes were to have opened Cantelli's 1956 Autumn season.)

November 29, 30.
Wagner A Faust Overture, *Ghedini* Concerto for Orchestra (first U.S. performance), *Brahms* Symphony No. 1.

December 2.
Brahms Symphony No. 1, *Ghedini* Concerto for Orchestra, *Wagner* Overture: Rienzi.

BOSTON
SYMPHONY
ORCHESTRA

All performances given in Symphony Hall, unless otherwise stated.
    Dates marked * indicate concert broadcast by WGBH, Boston. Dates marked ** indicate concert broadcast as above, but the first part also transmitted by NBC Radio network on Saturday evenings only.

1953
January 30, 31*.
Haydn Symphony No. 93, *Stravinsky* Jeu de cartes, *Rossini* Overture: Semiramide, *Tchaikovsky* Symphony No. 5.

February 3 Rhode Island — Providence.
Haydn Symphony No. 93, *Stravinsky* Jeu de cartes, *Rossini* Overture: Semiramide, *Tchaikovsky* Symphony No. 5.

February 6, 7*.
Frescobaldi/Ghedini Four Pieces, *Schumann* Symphony No. 4, *Busoni* Berceuse élégiaque, *Musorgsky/Ravel* Pictures at an Exhibition.

February 10. Connecticut — New London.
Haydn Symphony No. 93, *Stravinsky* Jeu de cartes, *Rossini* Overture: Semiramide, *Tchaikovsky* Symphony No. 5.

February 11. New York — Carnegie Hall.
Haydn Symphony No. 93, *Stravinsky* Jeu de cartes, *Rossini* Overture: Semiramide, *Tchaikovsky* Symphony No. 5.

February 12. Washington — Constitution Hall.
Haydn Symphony No. 93, *Stravinsky* Jeu de cartes, *Rossini* Overture: Semiramide, *Tchaikovsky* Symphony No. 5.

February 13. Brooklyn — Music Academy.
Haydn Symphony No. 93, *Stravinsky* Jeu de cartes, *Rossini* Overture: La gazza ladra, *Tchaikovsky* Symphony No. 5.

February 14. New York — Carnegie Hall.
Frescobaldi/Ghedini Four Pieces, *Stravinsky* Jeu de cartes, *Rossini* Overture: La gazza ladra, *Tchaikovsky* Symphony No. 5.

February 17*.
Haydn Symphony No. 93, *Stravinsky* Jeu des cartes, *Rossini* Overture: Semiramide, *Tchaikovsky* Symphony No. 5.

1954

March 26, 27*, 28**.
Andrea Gabrieli/Ghedini La battaglia, *Bartók* Music for Strings, Percussion and Celesta, *Brahms* Symphony No. 1

(This programme was repeated at Providence, but there is no performance date recorded in the orchestra's log of Cantelli's appearances.)

December 17, 18*, 19, 21**.
Verdi Requiem — with Herva Nelli, Claramae Turner, Eugene Conley, Nicola Moscona, New England Conservatory Chorus.

December 24, 25**.
Vivaldi Concerto Grosso Op. 3 No. 11, *Brahms* Symphony No. 3, *Respighi* Fontane di Roma, Pini di Roma.

December 28. Massachusetts — Cambridge.
Vivaldi Concerto Grosso Op. 3 No. 11, *Brahms* Symphony No. 3, *Respighi* Fontane di Roma, Pini di Roma.

PHILADELPHIA ORCHESTRA

Performance given at Philadelphia Academy of Music.

1949

February 25, 26.
Wagner A Faust Overture, *Brahms* Symphony No. 3, *Tchaikovsky* Overture: Romeo and Juliet, *Ghedini* Pezzo concertante, *Verdi* Overture: I vespri siciliani.

PITTSBURGH SYMPHONY ORCHESTRA

All performances given in Syria Mosque.

1951

February 23, 25.
Haydn Symphony No. 93, *Hindemith* Mathis der Maler, *Tchaikovsky* Symphony No. 5.

March 2, 4.
Schubert Symphony No. 2, *Rakhmaninov* Piano Concerto No. 1 — with Byron Janis, *Bartók* Concerto for Orchestra.

March 9, 11.
Vivaldi Concerto Grosso in A major, *Brahms* Symphony No. 3, *Sibelius* Violin Concerto — with Samuel Thaviu, *Busoni* Berceuse élégiaque, *Rossini* Overture: Semiramide.

SAN FRANCISCO SYMPHONY ORCHESTRA

Performance given in the Opera House.

1951

March 15, 16, 17.
Haydn Symphony No. 93, *Hindemith* Mathis der Maler, *Tchaikovsky* Symphony No. 5.

CHICAGO SYMPHONY ORCHESTRA

Performance given at Orchestra Hall.

1953

January 8, 9.
Haydn Symphony No. 93, *Hindemith* Mathis der Maler, *Tchaikovsky* Symphony No. 5.

VIENNA PHILHARMONIC ORCHESTRA

Performances given at the Salzburg Festival in the Festspielhaus.

1953

August 9.
Frescobaldi/Ghedini Four Pieces, *Schumann* Symphony No. 4, *Debussy* La Mer.

1954

August 8.
Rossini Overture: La gazza ladra, *Mendelssohn* Symphony No. 4, *Debussy* Prélude à l'après-midi d'un faune, *Ravel* Daphnis et Chloé: Suite No. 2.

PHILHARMONIA ORCHESTRA

All performances given at the Royal Festival Hall, unless otherwise stated.

1951

September 30.
Mendelssohn Symphony No. 4, *Tchaikovsky* Overture: Romeo and Juliet, *Busoni* Berceuse élégiaque, *Ravel* La valse.

October 3, 7.
Brahms Symphony No. 3, *Wagner* Siegfried Idyll, *Hindemith* Mathis der Maler.

October 10, 14.
Vivaldi Le quattro stagioni — with Manoug Parikian, *Strauss* Tod und Verklärung, *Sibelius* The Swan of Tuonela — with Peter Newbury, (cor anglais), *Rossini* Overture: Guillaume Tell.

1952

October 5.
Haydn Symphony No. 93, *Ravel* Pavane pour une infante défunte, Daphnis et Chloé; Suite No. 2, *Beethoven* Symphony No. 7.

October 8.
Vivaldi Concerto in A — with Thurston Dart (harpsichord), *Beethoven* Symphony No. 7, *Ravel* Daphnis et Chloé: Suite No. 2, Pavane pour une infante défunte, Bolero.

October 14.
Wagner A Faust Overture, *Tchaikovsky* Symphony No. 6, *Bartók* Concerto for Orchestra.

October 17.
Wagner A Faust Overture, *Schubert* Symphony No. 8, *Rossini* Overture: La gazza ladra, *Bartók* Concerto for Orchestra.

October 21.
Frescobaldi/Ghedini Four Pieces, *Frank* Symphony in D minor, *Musorgsky/Ravel* Pictures at an Exhibition.

October 23.
Frescobaldi/Ghedini Four Pieces, *Cherubini* Symphony in D, *Verdi* Overture: La forza del destino, *Musorgsky/Ravel* Pictures at an Exhibition.

1953

May 11. Royal Albert Hall.
Rossini Overture: Semiramide, *Schumann* Symphony No. 4, *Brahms* Symphony No. 1.
(This concert was dedicated to the memory of Dr. Chaim Weizmann [1874--1952], first President of the State of Israel, whose national anthem *Hatikvah* opened the programme. L.S. Amery also paid tribute to Weizmann. Broadcast — BBC Third Programme.)

May 14, Royal Albert Hall.
Berlioz Overture: Le carnival romain, *Tchaikovsky* Symphony No. 5, *Brahms* Symphony No. 1.

May 18. Royal Albert Hall.
Rossini Overture: Le siège de Corinthe, *Schubert* Symphony No. 9, *Beethoven* Symphony No. 5.

May 20, Royal Albert Hall.
Wagner Overture: Der fliegende Höllander, *Dvorâk* Symphony No. 9, *Beethoven* Symphony No. 5 (Broadcast — BBC Home Service.)

1954

May 23.
Rossini Overture: La cenerentola, *Beethoven* Symphony No. 6, *Debussy* Le martyre de Saint-Sébastien, La mer.

May 24.
Rossini Overture: L'italiana in Algeri, *Beethoven* Symphony No. 6, *Debussy* Prélude à l'après-midi d'un faune, La mer.

May 29.
Mozart Divertimento K.287, *Dukas* L'apprenti sorcier, *Tchaikovsky* Symphony No. 4.

May 30.
Mozart Divertimento K.287, *Falla* Suite: El sombrero de tres picos, *Tchaikovsky* Symphony No. 4.

September 9. Edinburgh Festival — Usher Hall.
Schumann Manfred Overture, Symphony No. 4, *Debussy* Le Martyre de Saint-Sébastien, La mer. (Broadcast — BBC Third Programme.)

September 10. Edinburgh Festival — Usher Hall. *Beethoven* Symphony No. 6, *Wagner* Siegfried Idyll, *Hindemith* Mathis der Maler. (Broadcast — BBC Home Service, Beethoven only.)

September 11. Edinburgh Festival — Usher Hall.
Tchaikovsky Symphony No. 4, *Musorgsky/Ravel* Pictures at an Exhibition. (An unbilled overture by Rossini opened this programme.)

1955

June 26.
Andrea Gabrieli/Ghedini La battaglia, *Beethoven* Symphony No. 8, *Debussy* Nuages and Fêtes, *Respighi* Pini di Roma.

June 28.
Mozart Ein musikalischer Spass K.522, *Beethoven* Symphony No. 1, *Debussy* Nuages and Fêtes, *Respighi* Pini di Roma.

July 1.
Vivaldi Concerto in D minor, *Beethoven* Symphony No. 2, *Casella* Paganiniana, *Ravel* Daphnis et Chloé: Suite No. 2.

July 3.
Geminiani/Marinuzzi: Andante — Strings, Organ and Harp, *Beethoven* Symphony No. 5, *Casella* Paganiniana, *Ravel* Daphnis et Chloé: Suite No. 2.

1956

July 1, 6.
Verdi Requiem — with Elisabeth Schwarzkopf, Ebe Stignani, Ferruccio Tagliavini, Giuseppe Modesti, Croydon Philharmonic Choir.

APPENDIX 2

THE RECORDINGS

Unless otherwise stated in the prefix listings, all recordings are 12″ LP.

In each discographical listing, the number given first is the original issue number. At the time of compilation, only those with the prefix SHB and SH are available in the U.K.

Apart from those recordings noted in context, all Cantelli's American recordings were made in Carnegie Hall. Session dates are given under each title.

U.K. record labels.
ALP — HMV
ASD — HMV Stereo
BLP — HMV 10″ LP
XLP — HMV Concert Classics
CFP — Classics for Pleasure
ENC — Encore (Defunct reissue series)
SREG — Regal Zonophone (EMI) Stereo
SHB — World Records (EMI)
SH — World Records (EMI)
7ER — HMV 7″ 45-rpm Extended Play
7P — HMV 7″ 45-rpm Single
DB — HMV 78-rpm
GBL — Philips Classical Favourites (Defunct reissue series)

U.S. record labels.
ANG — Angel (U.S. label of HMV) "S" denotes Stereo
SERA — Seraphim (Angel reissue series)
LHMV — RCA Victor (from HMV original recording)
LM — RCA Victor
DM — RCA Victor 78-rpm (Set numbers)
ARL1 — RCA Stereo
ML — Columbia (CBS)

Tapes
SBT — HMV stereo tape (7½ ips)
HTA — HMV tape (7½ ips)
TC/TC2 — World Records cassette

Beethoven Symphony No. 5 (2nd Movement only)
Philharmonia Orchestra/May 31, June 1, 1956. (For release details see under
The Art of Guido Cantelli.)

Beethoven Symphony No. 7
Philharmonia Orchestra/May 28–31, 1956. **ALP 1472 — ASD 254 — CFP
103 — SREG 2011** (U.S.: **ANG S 35260 — SERA S 60038**). Tape — **SBT
1254.** (This record is currently available in Italy on an Italian EMI historical
reissue label with the number **3C 053 01214.**)

Brahms Symphony No. 1
Philharmonia Orchestra/May 21, 22, 1953. **ALP 1152 — ENC 116 — XLP
30023** (U.S.: **LHMV 1054**).

Brahms Symphony No. 3
Philharmonia Orchestra/August 3, 9, 12, 16, 18, 1955. **BLP 1083 — XLP
30030**. Tape — **HTA 411**.

Busoni Berceuse élégiaque
Orchestra del Accademia di Santa Cecilia/May 10, 1949. **Unpublished —
Matrix numbers 2BA 6914/5.**

Casella: Paganiniana
Orchestra del Accademia di Santa Cecilia/May 13, 14, 1949. **DB 11334/5.**

Debussy: Le martyre de Saint-Sébastien
Philharmonia Orchestra/June 4, 8, 1954. **ALP 1228.**

Debussy Prélude à l'après-midi d'un faune
Philharmonia Orchestra (Gareth Morris — flute)/June 8, 9, 1954. **ALP 1207
— XLP 30092** (U.S.: **ANG 35525 — SERA 60077**).

Debussy La mer
Philharmonia Orchestra/September 13, 14, 1954. **ALP 1228** (U.S.: **SERA
60077**).

Debussy Nuages and Fêtes
Philharmonia Orchestra/August 3, 4, 6, 1955. **BLP 1089 — 7ER 5176 — XLP
30092** (U.S.: **ANG 35525 — SERA 60077**). Tape — **HTA 23**.

Dukas L'apprenti sorcier
Philharmonia Orchestra/June 1, 1954. **ALP 1207 — XLP 30092**. Tape —
HTA 23.

Falla Suite: El sombrero de tres picos
Philharmonia Orchestra/June 1, 1954. **ALP 1207 — 7ER 5057**. Tape — **HTA 23**.

Franck Symphony in D minor
NBC Symphony Orchestra/April 6, 1954. **ALP 1219** (U.S.: **LM 1852 — ARL1 3005** — first release in real stereo).

Haydn Symphony No. 93
NBC Symphony Orchestra/March 2, 1949. (Studio 8H.) **DB 21014/5/6 — DB 9477/8/9 Automatic couplings** (U.S.: **DM 1323 — LM 1089**).

Hindemith Mathis der Maler
NBC Symphony Orchestra/June 13, 1950. (Manhattan Centre.) **DB 21531/2/3 — DB 9765/6/7 Automatic couplings — BLP 1010** (U.S.: **DM 1407 — LM 1089**).

Mendelssohn Symphony No. 4
Philharmonia Orchestra/August 12, 13, 16, 1955. **ALP 1325 — SH 290** (U.S.: **ANG 35524 — SERA 60002**). Cassette — **TC-SH 290.**

Mozart Ein musikalischer Spass. K. 522
Philharmonia Orchestra/August 18, 1955. **ALP 1461 — XLP 30034.**

Mozart Symphony No. 29 K.201
Philharmonia Orchestra/June 2, 4, 1956. **ALP 1461 — ENC 122 — XLP 30034.**

Musorgsky/Ravel Pictures at an Exhibition
NBC Symphony Orchestra/January 23, 1951. **BLP 1085** (U.S.: **LM 1719** coupled with Romeo and Juliet/Philharmonia, see under Tchaikovsky).

Ravel Pavane pour une infante défunte
Philharmonia Orchestra/October 24, 25, 1952. (Royal Festival Hall.) (Dennis Brain — horn) **DB 21553 — ALP 1207 — 7ER 5057 — 7P 223 — XLP 30092** (U.S.: **ANG 35525**).

Ravel Daphnis et Chloé: Suite No. 2
Philharmonia Orchestra/August 4, 6, 1955, May 28, 1956. **BLP 1089 — XLP 30092** (U.S.: **ANG 35525**).

Rossini Overture: Le siège de Corinthe
Orchestra del Accademia di Santa Cecilia/May 9, 1949. **DB 11324.**

Schubert Symphony No. 8
Philharmonia Orchestra/August 18, 1955. **ALP 1325 — SH 290** (first release in real stereo) (U.S.: **ANG 35524 — SERA 60002**). Cassette — **TC-SH 290.**

Schumann Symphony No. 4
Philharmonia Orchestra/May 15, 21, 1953. **BLP 1044 — ENC 122 — XLP 30030** (U.S.: **LHMV 13**).

Tchaikovsky Symphony No. 5
Orchestra del Teatro alla Scala/September 23, 26, 1950. (Abbey Road Studios.) **DB 21187/8/9/21190/1 — DB 9583/4/5/6/7 Automatic couplings — ALP 1001 — SHB 52** (U.S.: **LHMV 1003**). Cassette — **TC2-SHB 52.**

Tchaikovsky Overture: Romeo and Juliet
Philharmonia Orchestra/October 13, 1951. **DB 21373/4/DBS 21375 single side — DBS 9705 single side/DB 9706/7 Automatic couplings — ALP 1086 — SH 287** (U.S.: **LM 1719 — LHMV 6028**). Cassette — **TC-SH 287.**

Tchaikovsky Symphony No. 6
Philharmonia Orchestra/October 24, 28, December 30, 1952. **ALP 1042 — SHB 52** (U.S.: **LHMV 1047**). Tape-**HTA 3**. Cassette — **TC2-SHB 52.**

Vivaldi Le quattro stagioni — with John Corigliano (violin)
New York Philharmonic Symphony Orchestra (Philharmonic on label)/March 1955. **GBL 3036** (U.S.: **ML 5044**).

Wagner Siegfried Idyll
Philharmonia Orchestra/October 16, 1951. (Dennis Brain — Horn) **DB 21478/9 — DB 9746/7 Automatic couplings — ALP 1086 — SH 287** (U.S.: **LHMV 13**). Cassette — **TC-SH 287.**

The Art of Guido Cantelli, a memorial to a great Symphonic conductor. (ALP 1535).
Philharmonia Orchestra: *Brahms* Symphony No. 3 — 1st Movement (from **BLP 1083**)/*Mendelssohn*: Symphony No. 4 — 2nd Movement (from **ALP 1325**)/*Schubert* Symphony No. 8 — 1st Movement (from **ALP 1325**)/*Tchaikovsky* Symphony No. 6 — 3rd Movement (from **ALP 1042**)/*Brahms* Symphony No. 1 — 3rd Movement (from **ALP 1152**)/*Beethoven* Symphony No. 5 — 2nd Movement

ALTERNATIVE DISCOGRAPHY

Over the past few years a number of recordings taken from Guido Cantelli's broadcasts have appeared on disc. Some of these are openly available from specialist dealers, others only by subscription to the issuing label. It must be remembered that, although these recordings are of supreme importance in supplementing Cantelli's commercial output, they are performances he did not approve for publication. Despite the admirable intentions of the people behind these Cantelli issues — and the vast amount of archive material now in circulation — this is no altruistic exercise. Without any payments being made for the use of this material, sales of "Pirate" or "Bootleg" recordings have reached a staggering total of thirty-five per cent of the American record market (this figure includes both pop and classical recordings) and with its present rate of growth the future development of the recording industry could be seriously undermined.

There is no way of knowing how much Cantelli material is taken directly from NBC and CBS master tapes of their broadcasts: NBC provided a minimal amount of information regarding Cantelli's work for them. CBS, however, maintained a comprehensive archive of their Philharmonic Symphony broadcasts until 1965, when they handed over to the Philharmonic whatever recordings they had of their broadcasts. The orchestra have not retained possession and have allowed the collection to become dispersed.*

There are no BBC or RAI transcriptions of Cantelli broadcasts. As a general rule of thumb, most of Cantelli's broadcast recordings are straight "Air Checks" — broadcasts taped directly off the air.

Of the NBC and CBS material, the Arturo Toscanini Society of America hold most of the NBC broadcasts and a great many of the CBS. Their issues are obtainable by subscription only, and they can be contacted at the following address:

The Arturo Toscanini Society,
PO Box 7312,
Burbank, Calif. 91505,
U.S.A.

The Society's issues form the widest selection of repertoire yet released and is presented in a series entitled "The Cantelli Legacy" of which two volumes are currently available.

The Cantelli Legacy — Volume One. **ATS-GC 1201–6.**
All performances with the NBC Symphony Orchestra. Broadcast dates are given after each item and the discs cannot be purchased separately.

---

*Information supplied by Bernard S. Krause, Director Operations and Business Affairs, CBS Radio Network.

Record 1: *Beethoven* Symphony No. 5 (February 21, 1954) This record also includes fragments of rehearsal taken from the aborted Philharmonia recording of the Symphony. Record 2: *Bartók* Music for Strings, Percussion and Celesta (December 13, 1952)/*Haydn* Symphony No. 88 (January 31, 1954). Record 3: *Beethoven* Symphony No. 1 (January 10, 1954)/*Schumann* Symphony No. 4 (November 29, 1952). Record 4: *Schubert* Symphony No. 9 (December 27, 1953). Record 5: *Tchaikovsky* Symphony No. 4 (February 14, 1954) This record also includes the interview with Ben Grauer mentioned in main biography. Record 6: *Weber* Overture: Euryanthe (November 29, 1952)/*Wagner* Overture: Rienzi (January 31, 1954)/*Ravel* Boléro (December 20, 1952)/La valse (February 7, 1954).

The Cantelli Legacy — Volume Two. **ATS-GC 1207-12.**
Details as volume one.

Record 1: *Bartók* Concerto for Orchestra (February 9, 1952). Record 2: *Tchaikovsky* Symphony No. 5 (March 1, 1952). Record 3: *Vivaldi* Concerto in A Flat for Two Violins — with Remo Bolognini and Daniel Guilet (December 6, 1952)/*Corelli* Concerto Grosso No. 8 (December 25, 1950)/*Geminiani/Marinuzzi* Andante — Strings, Organ and Harp (December 8, 1951)/*Vivaldi* Concerto Grosso No. 4 (February 2, 1952)/*Andrea Gabrieli/Ghedini* La battaglia (February 7, 1954)/*Gabrieli* Sacrae symphoniae: Canzona (February 16, 1952)/*Handel* Largo (December 27, 1953). The ATS notes give the broadcast date of the Handel as December 27, 1954 — a mistake. Record 4: *Rossini* Overtures: La Cenerentola (February 14, 1954)/Semiramide (December 4, 1950)/Il Signor Bruschino (with the New York Philharmonic Symphony Orchestra March 28, 1953)/Le siège de Corinthe (February 21, 1953)/*Casella* Paganiniana (January 10, 1954). The ATS notes give the broadcast date of *Il Signor Bruschino* as March 29 and the Casella as March 10, in both cases mistakenly. Record 5: *Cherubini* Symphony in D (December 27, 1952)/*Schubert* Symphony No. 2 (January 8, 1951). Record 6: *Britten* Sinfonia da Requiem (January 3, 1953)/*Barber* Overture: School for Scandal (December 20, 1953)/*Hindemith* Concert music for Brass and Strings (January 31, 1954).

The Cantelli Legacy — Volume Three. **ATS-GC 1213-8.**
Not yet available and programme subject to alteration. Details as volumes one and two, except that several Philharmonic Symphony performances are included.

Record 1: *Haydn* Symphony No. 93 (no date available)/*Hindemith* Mathis der Maler (no date available). Record 2: *Stravinsky* Chant du rossignol (no date available)/Fireworks (January 15, 1951)/Jeu de cartes (December 20, 1952). Record 3: *Tchaikovsky* Symphony No. 6 (February 21, 1953). Record 4: *Dvořák* Piano Concerto — with Rudolf Firkušný (January 20, 1952)/*Busoni* Tanzwalzer and Berceuse élégiaque (March 21, 1954)/*Falla* Suite: El sombrero de tres picos. The Dvořák and Busoni are with the New York Philharmonic Symphony Orchestra, no date or orchestra are available for the Falla. Record 5: *Mozart* Piano Concerto K. 467 — with Walter Gieseking and the New York Philharmonic Symphony Orchestra (March 6, 1955)/Divertimento K. 287 (no date or orchestra available). Record 6: *Beethoven* Piano Concerto No. 4 — with Wilhelm Backhaus and the New York Philharmonic Symphony Orchestra (March 18, 1956).

These ATS discs contain generous helpings of applause, enabling the listener to become caught up in the atmosphere of a Cantelli "live" performance. The NBC performances also contain Ben Grauer's opening and closing announcements.

Rococo Records Ltd, Box 175, Station "K", Toronto 12, Ontario, Canada.

Pizzetti Preludio ad un altro giorno/*Busoni* Berceuse élégiaque (March 21, 1954)/*Beethoven* Symphony No. 5 (February 21, 1954). **Rococo 2042.**

The Pizzetti and Busoni are with the New York Philharmonic Symphony Orchestra. Cantelli gave the first American performance of *Preludio ad un altro giorno* in the concerts on March 25 and 26, 1953, but it was not billed for the broadcast of March 28, and must have been included at the last moment. As can be seen from its date, the Beethoven Fifth is the NBC Symphony performance, here bereft of Ben Grauer's announcements. Sonically there is an opaque haze throughout this record, which makes the Pizzetti and Busoni rather more impenetrable than they really are.

Mendelssohn Violin Concerto — with Jascha Heifetz and the New York Philharmonic Symphony Orchestra (March 14, 1954). **Rococo 2071**

This record also contains Heifetz in live performances of works by Saint-Saëns, Korngold and Bruch (not conducted by Cantelli).

The Bruno Walter Society and Sound Archive, a Division of Educational Media Associates of America, Inc. P.O. Box 921, Berkeley, California 94701, U.S.A.

Mozart Piano Concerto K.467 — with Walter Gieseking and the New York Philharmonic Symphony Orchestra (March 6, 1955)/Piano Concerto K. 595 — Lausanne Chamber Orchestra (1948 — not conducted by Cantelli). **IGI 349.**

Mozart Così fan tutte. (Piccola Scala — January 27, 1956). **IGI 326.**

Apart from Cantelli's theatrical cuts, one number is missing from the tapes, from which this performance was transferred to disc. Following number thirty (Hawkes vocal score) which ends with Ferrando and Guglielmo echoing Don Alfonso's "Così fan tutte," there is applause leading into an eight-second break, during which you can clearly hear the tape cut off. The performance resumes abruptly on more applause mingled with laughter. This leads straight into the Allegro Assai of number thirty-one, the Act Two finale, beginning with Despina's words, "Fate presto o cariamici ... Missing is Despina's recitative between these numbers, "Vittoria padroncini!"

The recording is alleged to be taken from a broadcast but is not on a list of Cantelli's broadcasts supplied to me by the RAI. In Milan it was suggested that it may have come via a television set, as there were vague memories of the opening night being televised. It was certainly taken down by a recorder that suffers periodic bouts of wow and flutter, and my own feeling is that a recorder was linked into Piccola Scala's internal PA system, which would account for the sound being little better than a telephone line on a good day. Whoever acted as operator ran out of tape at the point mentioned and simply could not re-lace the machine in time. (This recording is also issued on: Cetra Opera Live — **LO 13**.)

Verdi Requiem — Boston Symphony Orchestra (December 17, 1954)/Te Deum — New York Philharmonic Symphony Orchestra (April 1, 1956). **IGI 340.**

There is a discrepancy between the broadcast dates as noted on the record label, and as supplied for all the Boston relays by the ATS. (This recording, minus the *Te Deum*, described as just "Boston 1954," is also issued on: Cetra Opera Live — **LO 503**).

Opus Records.

Mozart Piano Concerto K. 467 — with Walter Gieseking and the New York Philharmonic Symphony Orchestra (March 6, 1955)/*Bach* Italian Concerto — with Walter Gieseking/*Franck* Symphonic Variations — with Walter Gieseking and the Amsterdam Concertgebouw Orchestra/Mengelberg (taken from a 1940 broadcast). Opus Records — **MLG 70.**

Baton,
C/o, Historical Recording Society,
Box 1721,
Hamilton 5, Bermuda.

Strauss Tod und Verklärung — New York Philharmonic Symphony Orchestra (March 21, 1954)/*Bartok* Music for Strings, Percussion and Celesta — NBC Symphony Orchestra (December 13, 1952). **Baton 1005.**

No broadcast dates are given with this record. The dynamic range of the Bartok has been cut back to enable it to occupy one side, whereas the ATS disc of the same performance reproduces the mono sound with a range and clarity that puts it technically amongst the finest sound accorded a Cantelli relay. Unusually for a record from this source, the sleeve carries full programme notes. The Canadian pressings are extremely thin.

The records listed in this alternative discography, can only be a guide to what is available at the time of compilation, and by the very nature of their issue cannot be guaranteed to be readily available.

APPENDIX 3

THE INTERVIEWS

In the course of researching this biography, the following people took part in recorded interviews. Contributions other than in this form are noted in context. Recording dates are given after each name.

Marcello Abbado — May 20, 1978.
Luigi Alva — May 16, 1978.
Angelo Bernasconi — May 17, 1978.
David Bicknell — July 13, 1977. (Not taped.)
Leo Birnbaum — December 10, 1977. (Letter.)
Giuseppe Cantelli — May 17, 1978.
Iris Cantelli — May 12, 1978.
Mariangela Cantelli — May 17, 1978.
Dennis Clift — January 7, 1978.
Lawrance Collingwood — January 23, 1978. (Letter.)
Alfred Cursue — December 17, 1977. (By telephone.)
Arthur Davison — November 14, 1977.
Franco Ferrara — May 12, 1978.
Rudolf Firkušný — January 27, 1977. (Letter.)
Alfred Flaszynski — March 6, 1978.
Leslie French (By telephone.)
Giuseppe Gallini — May 22, 1978.
Hans Geiger — January 18, 1978.
Dr. Antonio Ghiringhelli — May 22, 1978. (Not taped.)
Charles Gerhardt — October 17, 1978.
Wilfred Hambleton — December 11, 1977. (Letter.)
Harold Jackson — January 10, 1978. (Letter.)
Cecil James — December 1, 1977.
Alexander Kok — July 23, 1977.
Jean Lefevre — Date unrecorded on transcription, during 1977.
Franco Mannino — May 10, 1978.
Igor Markevitch — September 3, 1977. (Letter.)
Gareth Morris — February 1, 1977.
Manoug Parikian — April 7, 1977.
Folco Perrino — May 17, 1978.
Clement C. Petrillo — July 12, 1978. (Letter.)
Clement Relf — October 9, 1977.

Max Salpeter — November 17, 1977.
Neill Sanders — November 22, 1977.
Graziella Sciutti — September 9, 1977.
Norina Semino — October 31, 1977.
Renata Scheffel-Stein — December 1, 1977.
Isaac Stern — February 8, 1978. (Letter.)
Sidney Sutcliffe — December 8, 1977.
Wally Toscanini — May 16, 1978. (Not taped.)
Antonino Votto — June 30, 1978. (Letter.)
Arthur Watson — July 7, 1977.
Marie Wilson — December 3, 1977.
Anne Wolfe — December 3, 1977.

BIBLIOGRAPHY

Bernard, Jack F: "Italy. An Historical Survey." David and Charles, Newton Abbot, 1971.
Boult, Adrian Cedric: "My Own Trumpet." Hamish Hamilton, London, 1973.
Cantelli, Iris: "Un Mucchio di Mani" (A Pile of Hands.) Samonà E Savelli, Rome, 1965.
Cassels, Alan. "Fascist Italy." Routledge and Kegan Paul, London, 1969.
Colonna, Luigi Sante: "Presenza di Guido Cantelli." Cura del Comune di Novara, 1962.
Marek, George R: "Toscanini." Vision Press, London, 1976.

INDEX

Abbado, Marcello 36-7
Alva, Luigi 106-8, 111, 117
Ansermet, Ernest 50, 52, 54, 100
Baxter, Sir Beverley 75, 121
Beecham, Sir Thomas 93
Bernasconi, Angelo 15, 17, 18, 22
Bernstein, Leonard 39, 54-5, 95, 121
Bicknell, David 58, 76, 103
Birnbaum, Leo 93
Böhm, Karl 108
Bolognini, Remo 53
Bori, Lucrezia 51
Bossi, Adolfo 25
Boulez, Pierre 100
Boult, Sir Adrian 69-71
Bradshaw, James 79
Brain, Dennis, 79, 89, 98-9
Brumaire, Jacqueline 111
Calabrese, Franco 107, 111
Callas, Maria 117
Cameron, Basil 73
Cantelli, Angela (née Riccardone) 14, 33
Cantelli, Antonio 14-16, 21, 33
Cantelli, Giuseppe 15, 18, 22
Cantelli, Iris (née Bilucaglia) 23-5, 33-5, 39, 50, 56-8, 62-3, 65, 77, 87-8, 103-5, 107-8, 115, 119-20, 122-3
Cantelli, Leonardo Guido 103, 105, 115, 120, 122
Cantelli, Mariangela 21, 63-4, 98
Cantelli, Sergio 98
Capuana, Franco 74
Carosio, Margherita 32
Chotzinoff, Samuel 50, 57, 59
Coccia, Carlo 11-13, 124
Coertse, Mimi 112
Corigliano, John 121
Cummings, Betty 62
Cummings, Jack 62-3
Cursue, Alfred 89
Davis, Bernard 102
Davison, Arthur 87, 105
Denison, Michael 46
Disney, Walt 46
Douglas, Keith 72
Eschinelli, Achille 23
Fasola, Felice 16-7, 23-5, 65, 117, 123
Ferrara, Franco 38-9, 41, 46, 117
Finamore, Concetta (Consolina) 120-1
Finamore, Nicodeme 120-1

Firkúsný, Rudolf 95-6
Flaszynski, Alfred 92
Fonteyn, Margot 112
Fournier, Pierre 113
Furtwängler, Wilhelm 87, 113
Gallini, Giuseppe 20, 26, 33, 35, 45, 49, 109
Gallini, Natale 19
Geiger, Hans 101
Gerhardt, Charles 100
Ghedini, Giorgio Federico 25-7, 33, 65, 117, 121, 123
Ghiringhelli, Dr Antonio 11, 36, 38, 46-7, 76, 105-7, 111, 116, 121-3
Gillis, Don 35, 66
Giulini, Carlo Maria 100, 123
Gobbi, Tito 46
Gorlinsky, S.A. 44, 78, 103
Grauer, Ben 66, 81
Harrison, Sidney 80
Hess, Dame Myra 72, 90
Hitchcock, Alfred 45
Horenstein, Jascha 112
Horowitz, Vladimir 52, 59
Horowitz, Wanda 50-1
James, Cecil 105
Karajan, Herbert von 78, 84, 107
Klemperer, Otto 90, 124
Koussevitsky, Serge 71
Krips, Josef 112
Lefevre, Jean 83, 104
Lipatti, Dinu 124-5
Lister, Moira 112
Luca, Giuseppe de 51, 60
Lucon, Arturo 13, 27
McCarthy, Joe 30
Maguire, Hugh 85
Mangiagalli, Riccardo Pick 36-7
Mannino, Franco 44-5, 64-5, 111
Markevitch, Igor 41
Marriner, Neville 85
Marshall, Lois 121
Mase, Georgina 77-8
Mase, Owen 69-74, 77-8, 80, 84, 89
Menuhin, Yehudi 112
Merowitch, Alexander 59
Merriman, Nan 107-8
Milstein, Nathan 50, 59
Miller, Frank 66
Minetti, Enrico 110, 114
Mitropoulos, Dimitri 94, 121

Mohr, Richard 61
Morris, Gareth 82, 92-3
Morris, Gwyn 80
Munch, Charles 51, 59
Mussolini, Benito 29-30, 34
Nelli, Herva 67
Neveu, Ginette 124-5
Olivieri, Piero 119
Orchestras:
BBC Symphony 69-72, 79, 86
Boston Symphony 60
I Musici 112
London Philharmonic 86
London Symphony 72-3, 112
Maggio Musicale Fiorentino (Florence Symphony) 40-1, 123
NBC Symphony 35, 45-7, 49-50, 52-4, 56, 58, 60, 63, 65-7, 74, 81, 85, 87-8, 98
New Philharmonia 100
New York Philharmonic Symphony 11, 17, 51, 54, 63, 79, 87, 94-6, 119, 121, 125
Orchestra del Accademia di Santa Cecilia 38
Orchestra del Teatro alla Scala 36-7, 75, 94, 117-8, 122-3
Orchestra del Teatro La Fenice 46
Philadelphia 59-61
Philharmonia 44, 77-84, 86-92, 94, 97-8, 100, 102-4, 107, 121, 125
Piccola Scala Orchestra 112, 114
Queens Hall Orchestra 86
Royal Philharmonic 87, 93
South African Broadcasting Corporation Symphony 112
Vienna Symphony 44
Virtuosi of England 87
Paray, Paul 121
Parikian, Manoug 79-80, 85-6, 88-90, 99, 104
Panerai, Rolando 107, 110-1, 117
Pedrollo, Arrigo 25
Perrino, Folco 17, 25, 32-3, 118-9
Petacci, Claretta 34
Petrillo, Clement 36
Pizzetti, Ildebrando 39
Quadri, Argeo 121
Relf, Clement 81, 85, 88, 101, 104
Rossellini, Roberto 33
Rota, Nino 46
Rubinstein, Artur 117
Sabata, Victor de 40-1, 74, 76, 107, 116, 122-3
Salpeter, Max 79
Sanders, Neill 91, 99
Sanzogno, Nino 107, 112
Sargent, Sir Malcolm 70. 73, 112

Scarpa, Sergio 21-2, 31
Scheffel-Stein, Renata 98, 104
Schwarzkopf, Elisabeth 107-8
Sciutti, Graziella 107-111, 115-7
Segovia, Andres 112
Semino, Norina 90-1, 105
Sinatra, Frank 54, 75
Somes, Michael 112
Stern, Isaac 95
Stokowski, Leopold 55, 58
Strauss, Richard 66, 71
Stravinsky, Igor 60
Strehler, Giorgio 107, 112
Swarowsky, Hans 121
Szell, George 94
Theatres and Concert Halls:
Carnegie Hall 55, 60, 65-6, 96
City Hall (Johannesburg) 113
His Majesty's Theatre (Johannesburg) 112
Piccola Scala 33, 105, 107, 112
Queens Hall 69, 72-3
Royal Albert Hall 75-6, 78
Royal Festival Hall 69-70, 73, 78, 82, 84-5, 89, 93, 98, 102, 104, 121
Royal Opera House Covent Garden 74-6
Sadlers Wells Theatre 72
Teatro alla Scala 11, 13, 20, 36, 38, 46, 63, 69, 74, 83-4, 88, 95, 102, 105-8, 110, 116-7, 119, 121-2, 124
Teatro Coccia 11-13, 20, 24, 26-7, 31, 33, 63, 117, 119, 123
Teatro La Fenice 39, 46, 49, 123
Teatro San Carlo 123
University Great Hall (Johannesburg) 112
Usher Hall 74, 94
Thurston, Frederick 79
Tornielli, Marquis Luigi 13, 124
Toscanini, Arturo 11, 21, 30, 38, 45-7, 50-67, 69-71, 74, 77-81, 83-8, 90, 94, 98, 105-6, 116, 122, 124-5
Toscanini, Carla 62, 70
Toscanini, Cia 52
Toscanini, Wally 124
Toscanini, Walter 45, 50-3, 59
Vecchi, Margherita de 51, 54, 56, 62
Visconti, Luchino 44, 106
Votto, Antonino 26, 36, 112, 117, 123
Walter, Bruno 71
Walton, Bernard 79
Watson, Major Arthur 40, 44, 74
Weingartner, Felix 71
Wilson, Marie 86
Wood, Sir Henry 71-3, 86
Zirato, Bruno 51